792.760

D0476783

RORY'S
STORY

Rory O'Connor is a stand-up comedian and the mastermind behind the phenomenally successful Rory's Stories. From its modest beginnings as a Facebook account where Rory would share anecdotes, skits and observations about life as a GAA supporter, today it is one of the biggest social media pages in the country. Rory has published two books of the best of Rory's Stories with Gill Books.

Dermot Crowe is a sports writer for the *Sunday Independent*. He previously wrote *Hell for Leather: A Journey Through Hurling in 100 Games* and contributed to a collection of essays, *Voices from Croke Park*.

LEABHARLANN
CO. CHILL DARA

RORY'S STORY

My unexpected journey
to self-belief

Rory O'Connor
with Dermot Crowe

Gill Books

Gill Books
Hume Avenue
Park West
Dublin 12
www.gillbooks.ie

Gill Books is an imprint of M.H. Gill and Co.

Text © Rory O'Connor
978 07171 89953

Print origination by O'K Graphic Design, Dublin
Edited by Djinn von Noorden
Proofread by Jane Rogers
Printed by CPI Group (UK) Ltd, Croydon, CRO 4YY

This book is typeset in 14/18 pt Minion

The paper used in this book comes from the wood pulp of managed forests. For every tree felled, at least one tree is planted, thereby renewing natural resources.

All rights reserved.
No part of this publication may be copied, reproduced or transmitted in any form or by any means, without written permission of the publishers.

A CIP catalogue record for this book is available from the British Library.
5 4 3 2 1

I would like to dedicate this book to anyone who is struggling, or has struggled, with their confidence and sense of hope. Trust your gut and believe in yourself.

Contents

Prologue

It's May 2013 and I'm walking the streets of Dublin in the rain. In a nearby bar the friends I came into town with earlier are still drinking. I'd made my excuses, pretending I was tired and needed to go home, and we'd parted company, when in reality it was all a big lie. I hurried to the nearest casino to gamble what money I'd left.

Why did I squander my last cent? There's no reason or logical explanation other than my senseless addiction. I never cared about the money I won; the thrill was always in the pursuit, the roll of the dice, the spin of the wheel. I had my first bet at sixteen, in Galway with my best friend Tony. We won. I can trace the roots of the problem to that exhilarating moment, but I also know it's not that simple.

A pastime that became a habit that became an obsession that veered out of control. I've never borrowed money to gamble; my losses were relatively modest compared to the high rollers, but it's been the source of enormous stress in my life that has brought me to my knees, sinking me into episodes of depression like the one I'm in now. I'm on this street feeling empty and worthless and I haven't the price of the taxi back home to Ashbourne. The rain falling on me is like a message from above.

There's a scene in *Trading Places*, the Eddie Murphy movie, where the successful guy who loses everything is on the street, hungry, humiliated, in a Santa suit, and just when it seems nothing can possibly get any worse, the heavens open. The rain buckets down on him and you can see he's on the brink. He takes a gun from his pocket, holds it to his temple and pulls the trigger. There's a click. The barrel is empty. He puts down the gun.

I'm 26 years old, in a job I've no heart for, with a partner and a child who rely on me, and I've just blown the last of my cash. All kinds of dark thoughts are entering my head. I need to get home. I'm miserable, defeated, demoralised. This can't be my epitaph. Because hard as it is to understand at this moment, the darkest hour is before the dawn.

A new chapter is about to begin.

PART 1

Chapter 1

Early doors

My parents are country people. Dad grew up on a farm in Offaly, but the land didn't keep him from uprooting in the early 1980s and moving to Ashbourne. He spent most of his life working in Dublin airport. A lot of my parents' friends would be rural people who came to live in Ashbourne and had jobs in Dublin. My father started off in Aer Lingus as a baggage handler. I remember lads asking me in school, 'Does your dad fly airplanes?' And I'd say, 'No, he'd be the other end of the spectrum.' But he worked hard, took chances and got promoted. And embedded into me was an impression of him not being afraid to take a risk or broaden his horizons.

I've early memories of Dad at parties where he'd be telling stories and have everyone laughing. I was too young to get any of the jokes, but I could see that people found him funny. He's a natural storyteller and that's obviously where I get it from. He has the gift of the gab. He's a brilliant singer but unfortunately, when he was about three, he lost the index finger on his right hand in a farming accident, so he can't play the guitar, but he can play the tin whistle and harmonica. Because of his own misfortune he was always at me to play the guitar, so finally this year I've taken the plunge. I'm going really well, taking lessons once a week. And that will hopefully become part of my act, finishing off a gig with bit of a song.

My dad's name is Michael, but we know him as Joe. I remember as a young lad seeing post addressed to 'Michael O'Connor' and thinking, who the fuck is Michael O'Connor? He's from a little place called Coolagh, which is on the Laois–Offaly border, maybe five miles from Geashill. He has nine sisters and two brothers – a typical hardworking rural family.

Some of my earliest GAA memories are of my dad bringing me to Offaly matches, going to Croke Park to see the great Offaly hurling teams of the 90s – the likes of John Troy, Johnny Pilkington, Joe Dooley, Johnny Dooley and Michael Duignan in full flow. I was seven when they beat Limerick with that spectacular finish. And of course, we followed Meath too, even though Dad was a blow-in and Offaly by blood and birth.

My dad can turn his hand to almost anything. He was caretaker in St Mary's school in Ashbourne for four years after he left the airport and no matter what you asked Joe O'Connor to do, he would fix it. I always wanted those skilled hands, but I just didn't have them. When I came home from woodwork class with a pile of shite, he always wondered why I couldn't do it when he could. Now I tell him, 'I might have got your bald head, but I didn't get your hands.'

Through his hard work he provided well for the family and my sister Carol and I were not short of holidays abroad. We went to Florida a couple of times, we went to Spain, I'd nothing but good experiences. And the number of times Dad bought me good golf clubs when I was younger and drove me to every corner of Meath when I was playing on the county underage teams. He was very proud of me playing county. Now he can be a stubborn man at times, he'll admit that himself – and I have that in me as well – but overall we get on well. We have a good relationship.

My mam, Marie Daly, is from a place called Collinstown in Co. Westmeath. She has three brothers and two sisters. She spent many years working for a catering company, so we got used to having minders when we were little. She and my dad bought a house in Castle Crescent in 1982 in an area of several converging housing estates known as Garden City. Carol was born on 7 April 1985 and I came along on St Patrick's Day, 17 March 1987.

My mam doesn't want to be mentioned in this book at all, but how can I write a memoir without mentioning my mother? She still goes to Mass each week. She loves her TV soaps. She just prefers a simple life. For years she watched me toiling, with few obvious prospects, and now that I seem to have found a clear track, I think she is happy for me and more settled.

My mother, like every good Irish mammy, did everything for me. Without her I would not have survived a lot of the scrapes I was in. I broke her heart countless times when I was growing up and caused her deep embarrassment, so everything I do, from now to the end of time, is driven by a desire to make her proud. She still watches me like a hawk – even the Rory's Stories videos, and the reactions they get. Typical mother, always looking out for you.

I don't blame her for being a worrier. I struggled badly in school and it was hard for my parents to see me making a career out of comedy when that started to become a more realistic ambition. As immensely supportive as my dad is to me – he still drives me to a lot of my shows – when the day came that I told him I was leaving my job to pursue Rory's Stories he sighed and said, 'Rory, forget about Rory's Stories, stick with your job.'

I always remind him of that, but I don't judge him. That is the way Irish people are and my mam and dad are the most cautious, stereotypical Irish people you will ever meet.

My dad was more nervous than me seeing me on stage when I went down that route. I remember him driving me to a gig in Limerick and he sat in the car for the whole thing, he wouldn't come in. I think he was terrified of me bombing and him not being able to do anything to help; also, he knows I'm liable to say anything. But then he saw me do a show in Sligo last year and that was a game-changer: he saw that I was doing alright, that I could handle it. He came away from that show and you could tell that he was pleased. He can't lie or hide his feelings. It's like whenever I had a bad match playing Gaelic football, he'd say it straight out. It was the same with the show. After the appearance in Sligo he said, 'Rory, I have to say, I was very pleasantly surprised.' I got a text off my mam before the show saying that my grandaunt Tess, who is in her early seventies, was going to be in the audience. That was a bit of worry given that some of the content is a bit racy. But it went fine. In fairness, a lot of my mam's side have been to the live show and they've really enjoyed it, which is great to hear – there are a few edgy parts that could offend some people.

I think that's that generation: they worry. They're always worrying about food, about money, about something. My mother could make a fry and leave half of it in the fridge for the following day. Wouldn't throw anything out. They were used to managing with less when they were younger and didn't waste food like we do now. They have carried all these things with them, and it shows in their behaviour and attitudes.

My sister and I are very different. Unlike me, she was a good student. People often couldn't believe we were brother and sister. Carol would have been quiet and reserved when I was loud and overblown. But we get on great. She's genuinely one of the kindest people in the world, probably too caring for her own good. She reads negative online comments about Rory's Stories and gets worked up despite me telling her to ignore them, they're just trolls.

She's so supportive of Rory's Stories. She tells me every day how proud she is of me. I don't like praise, believe it or not, it makes me feel uneasy, but she throws loads my way, especially with the mental health awareness work I do. She keeps reminding me that I'm helping so many others. Carol is a very encouraging and positive person in my life. She and Brendan (Bren) have one child, Scott, and now live in Ashbourne after spending a number of years in Australia.

From an early age I showed signs of an addictive personality. Having a serious asthmatic condition meant regular trips to Temple Street Children's Hospital – on one occasion my mam rushed me there in such a panic that she left her car outside the front of the hospital to save time. We were inside for a few hours and when we got back the car had been robbed and we were left stranded.

I had a few near misses. We had a great childminder, Nora (sadly, she has since passed away), who looked after us when we were little. During another severe asthma attack Dad was driving me to Temple Street and Nora was in the back seat. I was maybe one, if that, and she let out a roar in panic: 'Joe, he's gone blue … he's stopped breathing!' Poor Joe got a terrible fright, I'm sure, but I managed to survive that scare.

And that addictive nature surfaced through an almost manic reliance on my inhaler. When I started playing football the inhaler had to be with me. From the age of maybe eight to twenty, every time I was rained on, I got a chest infection. My immune system was the pits. Many matches were missed because of chest infections. I was even on antibiotics and not able to train and play at times when I was with the county under-21 team in 2007, the year our club won the intermediate championship. My chest really limited my time playing with the county.

A lot of people grow out of asthma, but I became totally fixated on the inhaler along the way. I could be playing a match and at half time, even if I wasn't wheezy, I'd have to go in and check my bag to make sure it was there. If for some reason I forgot the inhaler, I'd fear the worst. Even if I felt OK, I might have to be taken off ten minutes into the second half because my mind would be too distracted. I've often had managers go into the other dressing room and ask people if they had any inhalers they could lend me.

I remember one night when I was staying at Emma's house, before we moved in together, I was getting ready to go to bed when I looked in my washbag and to my horror discovered that there was no inhaler inside. Panic stations. Within ten minutes I'd convinced myself I was getting wheezy, so I got in the car and drove from Blanchardstown, where she lived, to my home in Ashbourne to get the inhaler.

My Uncle Breffni in Donegal is a kind of philosopher, a deep thinker. When I was in my teens, he often told me, 'Rory, come up to Buncrana and leave your inhaler at home and stay with me for three weeks and I'll get rid of that asthma.' I was too afraid to do it. And I'm raging that I didn't trust his advice because he was right – a lot of it was in my head.

It's an obsessive behaviour. Emma would often say that I'd be puffing my inhaler when there was absolutely no need. There are about seven or eight inhalers lying around my house at any one time. I won't go to bed unless the inhaler is beside me on the locker. Now my asthma is pretty much under control. It has its ups and downs, but I definitely don't need as many inhalers as I have.

The other indication that I have an addictive personality concerns a lifelong attachment to my teddy bear, which my Auntie Catherine gave me when I was born in the Rotunda. The teddy became a crucial and irreplaceable part of my life. Showing remarkable originality, I called him Ted. When I went to Offaly to visit my dad's relations, Ted was pillion passenger. When I went to Westmeath to the mother's family, Ted came too. When I was around ten my parents took Carol and me to Manchester. Mam wanted to get to see the set of *Coronation Street*. I headed to Old Trafford with my dad, because I was a Man United supporter at the time. We went to the stadium, did the tour, had a great time. Ted was there too of course. We had an early flight back and that night as I was going to bed, I turned to Mam and asked, 'Where's Ted?' We looked in the bag. No Ted. He'd been left behind in Manchester.

To say I had a breakdown is an understatement. You'd see less traumatic scenes from a heroin addict doing cold turkey. I did not stop crying. I didn't sleep all night. The next morning my dad said, 'Well fuck's sake anyway' and got on a flight back to Manchester to get Ted. I swear to god. Now he worked in Dublin airport and would have gone standby, but I still made him do it. Luckily Ted was still in the hotel in Manchester and we were soon reacquainted.

That's one of a few different hairy episodes of Ted going missing and me having a meltdown as a result. I don't know if you're born with this kind of addictive leaning and dependence or whether you develop it. But if you look at my antics around the inhaler and Ted from an early age, you'd have to concede that I was a prime candidate for an addiction to something more damaging in later life. Here I was going into national school and being the hard man in the class, bigger than everyone else, bawling my eyes out to get my teddy bear back. I remember lying on the couch aged 11, sucking my thumb, with Ted, and Mam saying, 'Rory, if anyone saw you now …'

Nowadays, Ted is in rag order; he's hanging together. My mam has sewn him back up a few times. There's socks stuffed up the poor hoor. I'd say about ten per cent of him is original, the rest is an assortment of other material used to patch him back together after years of wear and tear. Emma asked me what I wanted one time for Christmas and I said I'd like to have Ted repaired and restored to his former glory, and sure enough there is this place you can send your teddy to get it reconstructed but you have to sign a waiver in case something goes wrong along the way. I wasn't willing to sign. 'You're a weirdo,' Emma said, when she heard me explaining that this was a risk I wasn't prepared to take. When we moved into my parents' house recently while we were waiting to sort out a mortgage and she suggested we put Ted in a container, I laughed. Imagine! No chance. He has pride of place up in the bedroom.

There was one exception where I managed to break the habit. When Emma and I went to Australia for the best part of a year a decade ago, Ted didn't travel. I didn't want to take the chance of losing him. There was that and there was also a bit of Emma saying, 'Are you seriously bringing the teddy bear?'

Truth is, I want to be buried with this lad.

Ashbourne is home, and I'm probably a bit addicted to it as well. It's where I've lived for more than 30 years. Aside from that spell in Australia, I've never been away. Ashbourne is a Meath town that has grown and changed considerably during my lifetime, with many people relocating from Dublin city, which is within easy reach.

Being a relatively short distance from Dublin impacts the town in different ways. When I was playing under-10s our GAA club, Donaghmore-Ashbourne, entered the North Dublin leagues, so every Saturday we would play the likes of Erin's Isle, Ballymun and Whitehall. We didn't travel around Meath to play matches until we were a little older. In that sense we had a more intimate relationship with Dublin while never forgetting which side of the border we belonged to or where our true allegiance lay.

Even now people still think I'm from Dublin: 'Oh I thought you were from Dublin – you have a strong Dublin accent.' Before Rory's Stories I was always asked what part of Dublin I hailed from. No one I grew up with has a Meath accent and the Dublin influence is clear when they speak.

The demographic of the town has been altered by a huge population shift from the city and we are gradually adjusting to that. Now, at a guess, it's probably 70–30 in favour of Dubs over Meath natives – but it's still Meath ground.

In school there was a lad called Donal Caffrey who lived out in the Skryne area and who had an obvious Meath accent – the way he'd say 'How *are* ya?' in that drawl – like you'd hear from people around Navan. He was the only one in the class who spoke like that. And I wouldn't have one of the stronger local Dublin-sounding accents. Many of the people in the town who went to St Declan's National School with me moved out with their parents, their parents being true blue Dubs. But you'll find that any of the peripheral towns like Dunboyne, Bettystown or Ratoath will also have a strong Dublin element and the accents will have that unmistakable strain.

Like, I really noticed it when I started to play with the Meath under-15s. I became known as 'Big Rory from Dublin'. Now that really pissed me off and I had to 'sort out' a few lads because they annoyed me with that nonsense. It was only then I discovered, while playing with these boys from out the country, the difference in how we talked and they talked. *Jesus, they have some bogger accents*, I'd be thinking. Maybe it came from playing, even though only once a week, in the Dublin leagues. But they sounded very different to me even though we were all Meath players and committed to the green jersey.

To my ears the pure authentic Meath accent would be north Meath, anywhere around Kells, Nobber, that general area. A Meath accent, if you were to try and describe it, is where everything is *slowwwed riiight dowwwn.* Colm O'Rourke is a prime example. I have the character Eugene from Oldcastle in my show and he is based on that type of Meath traditionalist. Though I don't talk like that myself, I find it easy to do a Meath accent when I'm creating sketches because of my time playing football with lads from the country. You pick up their speech and their slang. You hear all sorts of things on a football field.

Growing up I was unusually big for my age, which had its pluses and minuses. I didn't blend easily into a crowd. For example, playing for Donaghmore-Ashbourne, everyone knew that I would be playing midfield, standing there like Gulliver, because I was so much taller than anybody else. When I played under-10 matches, the team mentors had to bring a copy of my passport to prove I wasn't too old. You'd have people in north Dublin clubs asking, 'Who the fuck is this banger?' I was the same height as the managers at that age. I was a bit of a freak, I really was, not far off six foot even then. To make matters worse for a fella who stood out, I have this protruding bone in my chest, and it was very noticeable then. This bone was more prominent when I was younger because I hadn't filled out. I hated playing on wet days because the jersey would stick to me and really highlight the bone, making me feel like a freak. I was often known as Rory from Ashbourne with the Bone. It gave me a bit of a complex and left me wondering what the hell was wrong with me. But the size was a family thing: Dad is 6'3" and well built, my grandfather was 6'6" in his prime, I've an uncle who is 6'5" and his son is 6'7".

At one stage I had an offer to join Ballymun Kickhams. Rob and Austin Healy moved out to Ashbourne from Ballymun when I was maybe in fourth class at St Declan's. We became pally straight away because a few years earlier we had played against each other when Donaghmore-Ashbourne faced Ballymun Kickhams in the Dublin leagues. That Ballymun team had Philly McMahon. Paddy Christie was the manager. There was also Davy Byrne, small in stature but what a warrior on the field. I think every team needs a player like Davy. Then you had Hubby, Alan Hubbard, and the Dolan brothers, players who went to the very top of the game. It was a serious team.

One day Austin told me that Paddy Christie was keen to get me to play for Ballymun. My head swelled up with notions of going off to pursue this glittering career, you know the way you are at 13 or 14 years of age. I'm thinking, *I've enough of my own club, I'm sick of winning the ball and kicking it into no one. I need to go somewhere I'll be appreciated.* So one day I went down to Ballymun with Austin and Rob to training and Paddy Christie was there and he said, 'Listen Rory, we're basically stuck for a big midfielder, we don't have anyone to win a ball. We have everyone else. If you're willing to come, I'll pick you up in Ashbourne and drop you back.' Ballymun had Adidas as sponsors at the time, so they had this savage-looking gear, they looked the business. It felt like I was being treated like a professional footballer. *Picked up for training!*

Before I even told my dad about being picked, I went to see Kathleen Tormey in SuperValu, where she worked. Kathleen was a prominent figure in the club in Ashbourne at the time, and what an incredible woman she was. For over ten years she battled cancer and had a tough time with illness. She passed away only this year during the coronavirus pandemic, which meant she couldn't have the send-off she deserved. But we lined the streets the day of her funeral, observing the required social distancing, in a final mark of respect.

Anyway, I went into Kathleen with the news of my exciting offer.

'Kathleen, I'm joining Ballymun.'

'Excuse me?'

'I said I'm joining Ballymun Kickhams, I need you to sign a transfer.'

'Rory,' she goes, 'you're not joining Ballymun Kickhams. Get a grip of yourself.'

I stormed out of the shop and went home and told my dad and if I thought Kathleen gave me a hostile response, by god my dad put the tin hat on it.

'If you think I'm driving you into Ballymun to play football, you may forget about it.'

So I picked up the phone and told Paddy Christie that I'd love to but that it was a non-runner.

And there's always been jokes that came out of that. I was at Philly McMahon's wedding recently and the craic we had with the likes of Ted Furman and Hubby, who were there as guests. 'Oh, you could have won a Dublin championship with us!' All this kind of stuff.

I don't regret that decision now because when it comes to your club there really is no place like home. My first two managers, who are still close friends, were Jimmy Walsh and Colm Menton. Colm was later a selector on minor teams and senior teams I played with and now that I'm back playing a bit of junior B this year Jimmy is a selector – so it's kind of neat that I started with him and am now finishing up my career with him there as well. Those are two great men: they just live and breathe the GAA. Every club has people like them. Colm's son Bryan is the current captain of the Meath senior team. That's great to see. For Colm to have a son captaining Meath is a dream come true. We slag Colm because he would talk a lot about Bryan but at the end of the day, he's dead proud of him and so he should be.

The GAA is always leading you down interesting roads. Only a few years after my failed move to Ballymun, Meath and Dublin were playing an under-16 match with Philly McMahon corner back and me in the middle of the field on the opposite side. And then fast-forward two years, I finish secondary school and go to Coláiste Íde to do a sports and recreational management course, and who's sitting in the same class but Philly. We became great friends. We would have palled around in the college and played football for the college team.

If you were to go back for a day to the class in Coláiste Íde and to look down the back of the room you'd have seen Philly with this kind of a mohawk blond thing on his head. Hard buck on the pitch but he fancied himself. He had the pink Timberland boots on, and he knew his style, he knew what he was about. He stood out. And you'd have seen that big lad at the back beside him. Then if you were told that in 14 years' time, on the same day, that that fella there was going to win a seventh All-Ireland medal with Dublin and that that fella beside him was going to perform to a full house at Vicar Street you'd have thought it was fairly far-fetched. But that's a fact, it happened, on the same day we did just that.

Chapter 2

Educate to liberate

School, from the beginning, felt like a jail sentence. Honestly, its only appeal was the chance to look at girls and have the craic. The only subject I liked was PE. I had no interest in any other subject. None. Even history would bore the hole off me. And if I ever wanted to know anything about history I'd ask my dad.

St Declan's Primary School in Ashbourne is a short walk from my home in Castle Crescent, but for much of my time there my mind was light years away. I never settled or felt at ease. It was a fairly raw establishment in those days and didn't have the best of reputations at the time. The principal, god rest him, was a bit soft, he let a lot go. Frank Reidy, a great Donaghmore-Ashbourne GAA club figure, took over when I left and he rejigged it and it is now probably the best primary school in Ashbourne. My daughter Ella goes there. But when I was a student it was rough and ready. Good guys and bad guys, you were one or the other. If you were bold you were out in the hall and that was it. We had one remedial teacher, Mary Curran, who was actually my next-door neighbour. Only the really, really bad learners went to Mary. She could only do so much – she was covering the whole school.

I had a hyperactive streak that made it hard to sit still for very long. I am sure if I was in school now, I'd be diagnosed with something, but back then you were thrown out: that's what solved the problem. I spent a lot of time out in the hall in St Declan's with Tony Morgan, a lifelong friend, who would also have been kicked out of class. And you'd just have the craic there all day. So I learned very little in school. I went to secondary school not being able to spell properly. And I still can't spell, even when I'm putting stuff up on social media. Hanging out in the hall in St Declan's, it could be a lonely place. Granted, I had my friends, Tony and Gary Lawlor and Gary McClean and Colin Sutton and Kieran Clarke, and we all had the craic with each other. But when it was only you down in that hall it was a very solitary place to be. Very rarely would a teacher come up and ask if everything was OK. That is how it was for me in the 1990s. You were just chucked out of class. You started to think that this was your natural place.

You'd want to do something very wrong to get suspended in primary school. I think we were in fifth or sixth class when a few of us, Simon Kerrigan, Philly Sutton and myself met up with Shane Nevin and went on the hop. We mitched off school that day and I might have robbed a few cigarettes off the oul lad. Shane had keys for the next-door neighbours' place, as he was minding it at the time and they were away, so we went up there to hang out for a while. It was then decided we would take the neighbours' car for a short spin. Shane, even at 11 a capable driver, took it around the block. Next thing the guards appeared. They rang the school and the shit hit the fan.

I have a lot of bad blood towards certain teachers. One in particular hated me: thought I was a gouger; that nothing was going to come of me. And it wasn't just me who thought this. I've spoken to teachers from that time who've said things like, 'Jesus, he was very tough on you.'

That particular teacher is partly to blame for my confidence issues, I believe. Like, one day a lad who would have been a messer said something smart to me out in the yard and I just grabbed him and gave him a knee and a dead leg. And he went bawling to the teacher. So there were 50-odd students there and this teacher made me stand up, which I hated because I was much bigger than everyone else. He said: 'Look at you, you're nothing but a big bully, you're an overgrown disgrace.'

I picked up the chair and I threw it across the classroom. And I walked out and home. Straight home to my dad, bawled my eyes and my dad being my dad stormed into the school and reared on him: 'How dare you look down on my son like that!'

We had a few good footballers, but the same teacher never started a GAA team even though it was obvious we were keen. 'How could I bring you gurriers anywhere?' he'd say. That was the usual excuse. He regarded the likes of me as a lost cause. I could see that even then. I could see that he figured I'd amount to nothing, that I couldn't be trusted. That I'd be a failure, nothing surer.

The only time I ever enjoyed primary school was when we played football among ourselves up in the back field once in a blue moon. There I stood out and dominated matches. For once I was in my element. I was good at something. That teacher never once said anything positive like, *You're a great footballer, Rory, if only you put that into the school.* There was none of that. He just gave up on me.

But there were other teachers who were very good to me. I still see them around now and you don't forget who was kind and considerate, who could see that I wasn't a waste of time and space. Some were kind but failed to understand or accept the fact that not everybody is going to be able to read at the same level, or do maths at the same level. It was very cut and dried with them. When you are not up to scratch you tended to be treated like a bit of a leper or outcast, shunted off to the side. All that can play havoc with self-esteem. When you are 11 or 12, you're very vulnerable. Your confidence is brittle. Teachers can make or break it.

I'd like to think that teachers now can reach out to all children. There might be a kid there who just doesn't understand what's going on. To me good teaching isn't about achieving excellent results with the brightest in the class – though that is part of it, of course. Like in football coaching, the mark of really good teaching is when you can develop and encourage those who are less naturally gifted. I mean, a football manager who inherits a richly talented squad of players has a clear advantage. But is he capable of nurturing the less able and making them better? Can he uncork that potential? That's what separates the good from the average. But first you have to identify those hidden talents and understand what makes the footballer or the student tick. The old way was to throw them out of the classroom if they weren't toeing the line.

From time to time my mam reminds me of a story. When we went on that trip to Manchester – the one on which I forgot Ted – we were on standby, which meant we were seated in different parts of the plane. For most of the journey over I talked to the man beside me. I would chat to anyone, I had no inhibitions that way. This man went up to the mother after the flight and said, 'That young man of yours is going to go far, I can tell you that now, I just know.' The man turned out to be the designer Paul Costelloe. But my mam must have despaired so many times in later years, and found little comfort or consolation in Paul's words.

When I was in fourth class my dad became so fed up with me getting all these bad notes and reports that he decided it was time we had a talk. So he sat me down with a piece of paper and sketched out a little diagram. Then he said: 'Right, Rory, this is a crossroads. To the left of this road is a good place, where good people go. Where you have a good job and you'll have a good house. That's the good part. Down the right-hand side, that's a bad road, that's where people end up on drugs and in prison. Now, Rory – what road do you want to go down?'

I looked at the lines on the page, then pointed to another route he'd drawn and asked: 'What's down that road?' And that's the road I went down, the unknown road. It was neither here nor there. A kind of no man's land.

I always had a habit of daydreaming. In school, particularly, I would often wander off into my own world. Then the teacher would shout out as I began to drift off, 'Rory, Rory, Rory!'

'What?' I'd reply, startled.

I might as well have been on a different planet. I would lose my train of thought very quickly. And I still struggle with that. As far back as I can remember I was having problems in school and much of that came down to a difficulty with learning and a giddy and exuberant nature. I was never malicious, a bad egg, I was just hyper and couldn't settle. That led me into trouble numerous times.

I think my reputation preceded me a little when I moved on from St Declan's to Ashbourne Community School. While primary school did have good moments, we never fully understood each other and when it was all over both parties were relieved to have gone their separate ways. Not being academic left me feeling isolated and often worthless. I am not going to pretend that I was an easy child to manage – I know I wasn't – but it was as if from an early stage a consensus opinion was formed on Rory O'Connor: that he hadn't much in the way of prospects; that he was a bit of an educational catastrophe. Part of the motivation for me writing this book is the impact of my experience of school and my absolute conviction that no child should be made to feel undervalued or alienated. Every child needs hope and encouragement to find out what they are good at. I believe everyone can contribute something useful. The trick is finding out what that might be.

If you did not fit a certain mould in school it was easy to fall away and become lost. I was never going to be a banker, or a solicitor or a doctor. I knew what I *couldn't* do. But what *could* I do? Who could tell me that? What I've become, the journey into a career in comedy, happened despite my experience of school, not because of it. Most days I came into class pumped up, that's how I was naturally. If I had a match in the afternoon then I'd be even more excitable because this was something to look forward to in school and that was a rare treat. I'd only have to get through two or three classes, then it would be into lunch and after that I was off playing football, which is what I enjoyed more than anything. I'd do impressions, maybe something off the guys in D'Unbelievables or the movie *Dumb and Dumber*, just trying to make the class laugh. It was a way of channelling energy, but it also unsettled the class and gave teachers headaches.

For the first three years of secondary school my partner in crime was Austin, before he left school to begin an apprenticeship as a plumber. We were like Bonnie and Clyde, always up to mischief. One day we had a free class and started writing under the tables, little inscriptions on Celtic and the IRA, whatever we thought was cool at the time. Two days later my future year head, Joe Gibney, who I got on well with, called Austin and me into his office and presented us with the charges. We denied all knowledge. Joe took us to down to the class and as he prepared to display the damage, he offered us one final chance at confession. Again, we shook our heads. 'Nothing to do with us, Sir.' So Joe flipped over a few tables and there it was, clear as crystal: *Rory and Austin woz ere*. That's how daft we were.

I enjoyed making people laugh in school. It made me feel a bit better about myself. I was doing it as far back as I can remember. Hanging around with lads that were older, there would be stuff I wouldn't get. People would be slagging me and I wouldn't realise, I was so dozy, letting on I got the joke even though I didn't have a clue. In a way, being hung out to dry like that gave me a grounding. I learned to laugh at myself. The key to making people laugh is to not take yourself too seriously, and I would never have taken myself seriously. I was well able to take the piss out of myself.

In school, a lot of the time, my concentration would go and next thing the need for attention or desire to kill boredom would take over. I'd make eye contact with one of the lads and fire a crayon across the room and put the head down when the teacher turned around to see who threw it. We'd get straws out of the local shop and blow bits of wet paper through them, aiming for the back of some unsuspecting innocent's head. And being exceptionally tall

Ashbourne Community School

Ashbourne, Co. Meath. Telephone: 01 835 3066, 835 3081/82. Fax 835 3083
Principal: Ciarán Flynn, B. Sc. M. Sc. O.C.G. H.D.E. Deputy Principal: Áine O'Sullivan B.A. H.D.E. M. Ed
E-Mail Addresses – Administration: ashcoms@indigo.ie Staff: ashcoms@iol.ie

23rd March 2001

Mr. &. Mrs. O'Connor
30 Castle Crescent
Ashbourne
Co. Meath

Re: Rory
Class: McAleese

Dear Mr. &. Mrs. O'Connor

Rory is being internally suspended on Saturday 24th March 2001 as a result of grafetti on school grounds

He should attend school from 9.00 am to 11.00 a.m. in full school uniform.

Suspension from school is a serious matter, it is reported to the Board of Management and is recorded in the minutes of the Board. In cases where further action is required to be taken, records of suspension are taken into account. The suspension can be appealed in writing to the Board of Management within a fourteen day period.

Following suspension, the student with parent/guardian must meet with the Year head and Principal/Deputy Principal. At this meeting, the student is required to present work completed while on suspension. It is the student's responsibility to obtain this work from class teachers.

Students must not return to class until this meeting has taken place.

Please contact the school to make this appointment at a mutually suitable time.

Le Meas,

P.P. Áine O'Sullivan

Ciarán Flynn
Principal

Printed on re-cycled paper

One of many letters that was sent home during my school days.

1, Deerpark, Ashbourne, Co. Meath.
Telephone: 01-8353066   Adult Education: 01-8353007 Fax: 01-8353083
Email: admin@ashcom.ie   adulted@ashcom.ie   Website: www.ashcom.ie

17th January, 2020.

Rory O'Connor

Dear Rory,

This year marks the 25th Anniversary of Ashbourne Community School and we plan to celebrate this milestone with an evening of music and reflection with past and current staff, students and parents.

This event will take place on Friday, 27th March, 2020 at 7.30 pm in the school's Sports Hall.

As a past pupil, we would be delighted if you would attend and speak on the night about your time in the school and how it influenced your life. For those involved in the school for the past twenty five years, it will create a great opportunity to meet up and share memories.

I would be grateful if you could advise me if you are available to attend.

Yours sincerely,

Susan Duffy,
Principal.

Principal: Susan Duffy, B.A., H.D.E., M.Ed.
Deputy Principals: Ciarán Stewart B.Sc P.G.C.E. M.Ed
                     Pat Moriarty, T.Tech (Ed)
                     Gillian Casey, B.A., H.D.E., M.Ed.

A letter from the current principal of Ashbourne Community School, inviting me to come back and speak about my journey. Two letters, eighteen years apart, each with a very different message.

for my age, I was easy to pick out if the teacher was looking for someone to blame. When the teacher heard a noise and turned around, who was the first person to catch his eye but yours truly. Maybe I just looked like trouble. It was not unusual for me to be confused with one of the teachers – Joe Gibney actually thought I was a teacher on my first day.

When I was struggling in school, I kept telling myself that I'd find something and that's what kept me going. I remember having rows with my mother, saying, 'Mam, trust me, I'll be OK!' I knew deep down I had something there. I always knew; it was pure instinct. I knew I had the potential to be someone special. I can't explain how or why. But it was difficult during those days when nobody encouraged you to believe in yourself or to pursue what you felt deep inside your gut. You were just seen as giddy and misguided, a bit of a fool.

The most infamous episode I was involved in took place when I was a third-year student at Ashbourne Community School. One day Austin Healy and I were thrown out of class and placed on litter duty. Our first call on this clean-up mission was the toilets. I'd interrupted my cleaning to have a pee when Austin came up behind me and hit me a big shoulder. I'd a new jacket at the time. When I got back on my feet the jacket was covered in piss. I flipped. I ran into one of the cubicles and spotted a big shite left unflushed. I fished it out using the pickers we had for the litter collection and fired it at him in pure temper. It made a bit of a mess. And then I chased him up the corridor. I just lost it.

The school authorities were alarmed and straight away I was suspended for two weeks. They wanted to expel me. They thought I was psychotic. The only reason I was allowed back into the school was because I agreed to see a psychiatrist to prove that I was fit to continue my education. That's how seriously they treated the incident. All kinds of rumours went around the school that I'd crapped in my hand and threw the results at Austin. The story grew wings. The first day back and someone said, 'Ah, Rory, don't shite yourself today.' And it felt horrible. It didn't feel like something I wanted to laugh or joke about. That was not how it happened and I didn't want to be seen in that way. Because it wasn't me.

My mam was only too used to getting calls from the school after situations I'd been caught up in or engineered. I'd be outside my Year Head's office and he'd be going, 'Hello Marie, it's me again. Look Marie, I'm going to have to send Rory home again ...'

But this time it was different. There were people who felt I should not be allowed back. I believe Joe Gibney was the one who managed to persuade them to keep me in school, not to have me expelled. He tried to explain that a lot of this behaviour was down to me being a bit hyper but that deep down I had a good heart. That it was worse than it looked. So I agreed to go and see this psychiatrist. And it was exactly as you'd expect.

'Rory, when I say "mountains" what do you think?'

'High.'

I gave honest answers, and I spoke about myself, my feelings about school and the difficulties I was having. And he did up his report for the school with certain recommendations that he felt would help me settle in better. The letter from the psychiatrist is still at home. He summed me up as a highly energetic young lad but certainly not psychotic or deranged. He recommended that I be removed from Irish class. He recommended the Leaving Cert Applied rather than the Leaving Cert. I went back to school and sat eight subjects for the Junior Cert that year, a couple below the average.

I know I broke my Mam's heart. Like I said, she doesn't like too much attention, she keeps everything to herself. All her family are very down to earth. The Daly and O'Connor families are chalk and cheese. My father's family have a bit of craic and madness in them while the Dalys are more reserved, old school and down the middle. And all of my mam's sisters' children went to college and all of a sudden along comes this square peg in a round hole called Rory. When it was decided that I would sit the LCA rather than the Leaving Cert I'd say she was conscious of me lowering the bar. How was she going to explain this to my relations, who were all high achievers? Even my daughter Ella enjoys school. She comes home and says, 'Mam, can I do my homework before I go out?' I would have burnt my schoolbag before I'd have said something like that.

When I got into trouble she'd just go silent. That was the worst. I'd rather a verbal attack from my father any day of the week over my mam giving me the silent treatment because I knew that that's when she was low. She'd tear up and say something like, 'I am very disappointed in you, Rory,' and that would have made me feel shit.

After attending the psychiatrist, Irish was a cross I no longer had to bear: whenever Irish was on I just went to Miss Meade's room and waited there. I did alright in the Junior Cert exam, passed all the subjects, with two honours. I did as well as the average Joe. And Miss Meade was a good support to me in those years, as was Declan Sheeran, my science teacher. He realised that I was struggling and gave me extra tutoring. Now, he ended up marrying Miss Meade, so maybe he had an ulterior motive when he was dropping by to help me out, but I still can't say a bad word about him. But despite their help I felt down when I didn't understand what was going on, which was most of the time. I would continue to distract others in the hope that they might not notice that I wasn't grasping what the teacher was saying. From an early stage I had just accepted that I was stupid.

Chapter 3

Street life

LEABHARLANN
CO. CHILL DARA

Towards the end of primary school and through my early teenage years, a gang began to hang out around Garden City. I suppose we would have been known as troublemakers, because it looked like we were up to no good – and sometimes we were. But at that age a group dynamic can take on a life of its own and you're swept along. There was no harm in what we did most of the time except to ourselves and our reputations. We would assemble at the shops just below St Declan's, smoke a bit of hash and drink a few cans, from the age of about 11 to 15. That's what we did each weekend.

On Friday nights we'd hang around the shops until we persuaded someone to buy us cans. I'll always remember standing at the bushes, heart racing when you saw someone coming around the corner with two big bags of Dutch Gold. I usually got six cans, some of the boys would take ten, then we'd get a lump of hash and head up to the fields and spend an hour or two there. You might drink two or three cans and you'd open another and say, 'Boys, I am going for a piss,' and then pour that out in the ditch. I think everyone did that. You didn't want to be too drunk.

There was a drink mixture we used to call bombshell. I'd sneak into the drinks press in my house and get a plastic bottle and take a little bit out of the whiskey, a little bit out of the wine and mix it up and that would fuck you up. Often puked me ring on those. Some days you'd wander in and sneak up to bed and other days the mother would catch you out and you'd be grounded.

My cousins Tim, Ross, Breifne and Barney were a year or two older than me, but we were all close. During family parties down in Auntie Jenny's house we'd rob a few cans and drink them up in the room. I would probably only have been 11 at the time. On a few occasions my mam would have smoked us out and given me a telling off. They were strict enough, my parents, but I still did it anyway. I used to plead with Mam not to tell Dad: he's a big man and would never hit me, but I was afraid of him. When he got angry he'd wake a corpse.

One early brush with the law proved that I would never be a successful drug dealer. One evening we were smoking joints near the school, and while I was rolling one under the street light I heard Simon and maybe Niall, who were at the shops, suddenly yell, 'Rory, Guards!'

I have what's called a 'five-second brain', in that it takes me five seconds to register what someone has just said. I saw this garda car and threw the joint over my shoulder. The guard got out of the car and came over.

'What did you throw?'

'I didn't throw anything!'

'If I shine my light are you telling me I won't find anything?'

'Yes!'

He shone the torch in the general area where it had landed. My heart was thumping. Next you see this big nappy of a joint. It wasn't easy to miss: I was never good at rolling them, I had big fat fingers. The guard picked up the offending article. 'What's this?'

'It's not mine.'

I heard the boys pleading, 'Rory! Will you run?'

The guard asked me for my name and address and, having given him my details, I ran for it.

I ran like I never ran before. I even remember the route I took. I jumped this wall, I don't know how I did. They often say the body is at its fittest and most able when you're running from the guards. This adrenaline rush comes over you. But in jumping the wall I burst my ankle. My whole body went numb from the ankle injury and after all that effort and heroics, when I got home, who was at the door? Only the guards. I remember walking in and saying, 'Do you mind giving me five minutes to tell my ma how much I love her and that I'm sorry before you arrest me?' I was probably only 14. The garda was a local, so after a bit of talking and a full confession, I got away with a clip on the ear.

But trouble was never far away – both out of school and in it. One day, around third year at secondary school in

Ashbourne, Tony and I were just after finishing a joint. I had about a tenner's worth of hash in my pocket and as we're walking into school, we're met by Miss Meade, the remedial teacher, who has the two of us in her class. 'Rory, can I have a word with you?' she asked. 'You're not dealing drugs, are you?'

'What? No!'

'Like, are you sure? I've had a report that you are, so just giving you notice that the year head is going to be looking for you.'

I went into Ms Mulvey's class. My heart was thumping. I was shitting myself. I threw the hash in a bin on the way to class. Next thing the year head comes in. And he was a tough cookie.

'Sorry for disturbing you, Ms Mulvey, can I have Mr O'Connor for one second?' He looked at me. 'C'mere you!'

Oh my god, I thought, *I'm dead.*

He walked me around the corner and kinda pinned me against the wall and said, 'I fucking knew the day I set eyes on you that you were trouble.' Then he mentioned a teacher in primary school who had warned him about me, saying that this teacher was dead right in what he'd said. 'You're dealing drugs and I'm going to have you expelled from this school today,' he hissed. Then he let me go and walked off.

That day we had a match. Mr Moriarty and Mr McIvor, who I'd great time for, were the joint managers. They were really good teachers who understood the type of person I was. I went straight to Mr Moriarty and told him I wouldn't be able to play the game and that I thought I was going to get expelled. So, long story short, there was a meeting called and Joe Gibney stood in and said, 'Listen, Rory has to come and play this match.' I was the team captain, so an important player – he gave it all that. It was like the quarter final of a Leinster schools competition.

I had one of the best games of my life because it was an hour or two of bliss where I could escape the reality of the serious trouble I was in. I was so grateful that I played out of my skin. I couldn't do anything wrong on the pitch that day. But the minute that final whistle went I knew it was time to face the music.

A meeting was held between my parents and the school. My mother was in the parents' association and she was very embarrassed by this. And my dad was mad to get me home and, like, he'd never physically beat me up but I could see he was raging. I pleaded my innocence – told them that I never dealt drugs.

It was revealed later that the partner of one of the second-year teachers had seen me with the lads from Youthreach – the school leavers' programme – and noticed a joint being passed around and that's where the accusation came from. I smoked a bit of hash, admittedly, but I never sold any. So that's how the story came about. Someone added two and two and got five.

I was suspended for a week and it soon blew over. Once again, I managed not to get expelled. In a way you kind of accepted that, well, you were a bit of a bowsie and this is how bowsies go on. But I knew in my heart and soul I wasn't a bad person. There was no harm in me. I just needed direction. I needed someone to say, 'Listen, let's have a chat.'

I recently did a talk in a school in Donegal where the principal is a man called John Gorman. He invited me up because he is the kind of man who thinks a little differently. For one thing he believes that no student should be expelled from school; that there is no student who is a lost cause. John thinks that there should always be an alternative option for them. He sent me a message and straight away I decided that I was going up.

The message I gave the students was simple enough. Don't allow yourself get bogged down if you don't understand what is going on in the classroom, it's not going to define you. If you do understand what is going on in the classroom, well, then push yourself – don't be afraid to be a geek. It's like a footballer who knows he can catch a ball and kick it over the bar but won't because he doesn't want everyone else to feel a lesser footballer in comparison. If you know the answers you tell the teacher the answers.

Many of the lads who hung around with me at school are doing well for themselves now. Simon is a qualified mechanic in Australia. Conor is a qualified electrician. Niall is a quantity surveyor. They all broke away because they were all good lads. Shane is still lorry-driving. Tony is a block-layer. When I stopped hanging around the shops the only person I really missed was Tony because we got on so well. He left school in third year to become a block-layer and was earning well so he started going on mad sessions on a Friday night, drinking vodka and Red Bull and all. I'd go down the village to get a takeaway or a video and see Tony, who was 16 or 17 at the time, outside the pub in his working boots, pissed drunk. 'Tony, do you want to come back to my gaff?' I'd ask him.

'No, fuck off, I'm on the beer.'

He would often knock on my door on a Sunday morning after a heavy night at a house party. And I would bring him in. I'd let him thaw out in the front room. Often I'd get a phone call from his mother, Theresa, crying. She was a great friend. Theresa and her husband Noel have three children, Tony, Dave and Denise, and Dave, like Tony, would be a valued friend.

I knew there was a lot of good in Tony and eventually he broke away from that too and found his feet. He built his own house, had a lovely daughter, Emily, my godchild. A lovely wife in Jen. He lives out in the country outside Ashbourne. We talk at least twice a week on the phone.

Life can go either way and you need luck at times to survive. On the August bank holiday in 2016 we were all out one night for Adam Fitzgerald's 30th – he was home from New York – and later that evening Tony suffered a serious beating. On the way home from a nightclub he got jumped on by four lads. Next day I went to see him in hospital. He was as good as dead. Bleeding in the brain. Jen was desperately upset. She'd got punched in the head that night as well.

He lost his sense of smell and was out of work for a long stretch, so he had no income. I feel I know him as well as anyone and he wasn't himself for a long time. Tony is one of the hardest lads you will ever meet, but it was a brutal attack.

I suggested that we do a little fundraiser for him, a gig in the local GAA club. I hadn't done a local gig for a few years. We put it on and people were very supportive. We might have made ten grand. That got them through the period while he didn't work and it felt great for me that I was able to use my name to help a friend, even though the name wasn't that big then.

Another fella I knew from childhood wasn't as lucky. Barry Maguire was known as Gump, and sometimes we called him the 'white Tupac'. He was a bit of a mad bastard but I loved him. Madder than any of us and a real diehard Meath man. When I started playing for Meath he would have been one of the lads I was drinking cans with and he'd be saying, 'Rory, you need to break away from this if you want to play for Meath.' He was a great footballer himself, but he was sent off most times he played because he was a loose cannon.

In the early hours of St Stephen's Day 2007 there was a bit of a row outside the Milltown estate. Lads with machetes came running from houses. Gump was at home but someone alerted him and he left his house and sprinted down and started throwing digs and before he knew it the knife was in him. Another lad, Damien Carthy (Dick), was also stabbed but survived. Stephen Kavanagh (Bic), a good friend of mine, was there and tried to comfort him until the guards came but Gump didn't make it. He died aged just 23. Bic had been playing poker in my house only hours earlier. That still sticks with me. Even when I'm doing Rory's Stories I often think, *what would Gump do*? He had that no-fear attitude. Whenever I'm nervous at a gig, I think of Gump and how he'd just pile in there.

The last time I made contact with him was in the GAA club and I wish it had been a better encounter. He had a bit too much drink on him and one of the officers saw him and said to me, 'Rory, you're going to have to ask that man to leave.' And I had to put him out of the GAA club. I never saw him again. That hurts.

I was madly hungover when the doorbell rang the morning of the attack. My father answered the door and I came crawling out of bed and sat at the top of the stairs. It was Tony. 'Ah Tony, the whiskey,' I mumbled.

'Did you not hear? Gump is dead and Dick is on a life-support machine.'

When we walked down the street a bit later it was all sectioned off by the guards. It was St Stephen's Day. The story was on the news. It was all very surreal. We always think of him around Christmas. A lot of people miss Gump. He was known as a troublemaker, but I knew there was a good heart in him, like a lot of people who have potential to make a better life for themselves if they are given a chance.

After the Junior Cert I became one of a group of around 15 students who followed the sign saying Leaving Cert Applied – just like the psychiatrist had recommended. You had an unbelievable array of characters in the one room. Owen Andrews ('Snako') came from Gormanston to Ashbourne in third year. I got to know him through the football team. After fifth year I persuaded him to come back and do LCA, told him that it was great craic, and not to mind that Leaving Cert. So Snako joined the LCA crew – now I don't know if he thanks me for that. There was Philly Sutton. You had the Milltown girls, as we called them, from a council estate in Ashbourne – I have so many close friends from there. Others included Ciaran Molloy, who is a butcher in Ashbourne, and Eoin Carey, who works in Dunnes, and Kingsley Ischei, originally from Nigeria.

We spent two years in each other's company. And we had slightly different rules to the others in school. You had more freedom. You weren't turfed out of class. Mr McLoughlin was one of our tutors and he treated us like adults. And Caroline Matthews, our tutor for sixth year, helped as well, allowing the students a little more pride in themselves. She was great. If I was getting too hyper, Caroline might tell me to take a break and go for a walk. She understood me.

Often on a Monday morning we'd be in class and the Milltown girls would have been out on the Sunday night in a local nightclub and they would come in, eyes hanging out of their heads, and I'd be going, 'Ah, Clare, I heard about you last night! The boys were telling me.' I loved winding them up. On a Friday with 20 minutes left in the day and nobody arsed doing anything Caroline might say, 'Sure, sing us a song, Rory.' And I'd belt out 'Raglan Road' or 'The Streets of New York'. I was offered an audience, was made feel a bit more important.

There was a stigma to it of course. We were still the LCA heads. We knew that. We'd have been regarded by some of the other students in school as lost souls, on a ship doomed for the rocks. When we had our final graduation Mass before leaving school, they called up the different classes. It came to our turn and you got the feeling that people were thinking, *Oh here's the rejects.* Before it all finished, I was called up to sing 'Raglan Road' in front of a packed church. That's how I signed off from school, at least on a positive note and striking a bit of a blow for the LCA students. I knew there was so much potential in everyone in the LCA class but some of their lives later spun out of control. So when I do school talks now I speak to LCA students and say that they should not allow others to set limits on what they can do.

I loved a bit of mischief, though. No denying that. I once managed to spark a fight between Wayne, the second-biggest in the class after me, and Kingsley, by telling each of them that the other one was going to bate the head off them. They both agreed to fight and I announce to all that there's a contest at lunchtime. Out we all head to the yard. Wayne is standing there, doing a bit of shadow-boxing. It was mid-November, freezing weather. And Kingsley comes around, rips off the top, rips off the shirt, bare back, and floors Wayne.

Joe Gibney comes in and pulls them apart. 'Back to class, everyone!' Then he calls me into his office. 'I believe you're the Don King, Rory, are you?'

Joe got me. He knew the type of character I was, knew that school wasn't my natural habitat. He was a maths teacher, didn't have me in any of his classes, but he was my year head for fifth and sixth year in LCA. Joe came from Oldcastle, a diehard Meath man. When I was younger I had a marked physical edge on the football field and I could throw my weight around. He loved that. He was very proud when I started making the Meath underage teams. When I was struggling in school and running into trouble, football offered me a lifeline and kept my head above water. Often, when I'd be kicked out of class, I'd go to Joe's room and he'd say, 'Ah, Rory, don't be an eejit.' He'd give me a small telling off. And then we'd talk about football. 'So come here, tell me about the football.' That's the way it always was with Joe.

Caroline Matthews was another positive influence. In hindsight I started my comedy trade in school because she encouraged me to tell stories in class and make people laugh – I was already developing the ability to talk in front of an audience. She never told me to shut up. She'd always laugh with us. She was brilliant. I mean through all the tough times when I felt lost and marginalised, there were moments like those where Caroline was just being kind and accommodating and it was worth more than she'll ever know. She always brings me back to give talks. She is delighted at how I've turned out.

But probably the biggest influence on straightening me out during my teenage years was football, and especially getting on the Meath underage teams. Once Meath entered the picture football took over much of my time. I started to look after myself more: eating better, training harder and drinking less. Another local player, Niall Farrell, a year older than me, was on the county minor team and I could see that he was not interested in any of that weekend drinking, which rubbed off on me too. Without realising it I was gradually breaking away from the lads I had messed around with, loosening that connection. But I don't regret any of those times, not most of them at least. We had a lot of fun and great friendships that have lasted the test of time in most cases.

Now when they were drinking cans on a Friday and Saturday night I would have been staying in because I had a match with Meath. The odd time I might go out with them and have a can and go home. Conor could drink 12 cans and he'd tell you the alphabet backwards and some other lad would have three cans and be fighting with himself having a piss. Some of the lads would have been dabbling in the ecstasy then. I never did, though I came close once. I was smoking from around ten, not good for a lad with bad asthma. My dad used to smoke Rothmans, which would burn the lungs out of you. I'd find some ends in the ashtray and smoke what was left of those. Now I only smoke socially, if even that.

In my teenage years I found that golf, like GAA, also got me into a routine and taught me a level of discipline. My dad played a good bit and all my cousins in Firhouse, the O'Connors, they're all savage golfers, low handicaps. I spent many a summer on the local pitch-and-putt course, and I represented Meath in Community Games in Mosney in pitch-and-putt. Me and Fintan Bonner, Damien McCartan, Breffni Conaty, Peter Milner, Barry McCarthy and Robert Smyth, we were the original juniors of Ashbourne Golf Club.

Physical exercise, such as playing football, was better than any therapy for a guy as hyperactive as me, offering a release for any steam that needed to be let out. In recent years I have become a big fan of the boxer Tyson Fury, who swears by exercise as a means of maintaining a healthy mind. There are so many people out there who use physical exercise to keep their head in a good place.

The GAA became an anchor during my teenage years at times when I could have totally lost my way. Various people in the GAA became my role models – I wanted to emulate them. I had seen Meath win the All-Ireland in the 1990s as a young lad and lads like Trevor Giles and Graham Geraghty and Paddy Reynolds coming to the summer camps. That all inspired me. Hanging out at the weekends drinking cans started to become less interesting when I got on the Meath under 15-team. Going down to train with Meath, and I suppose that first time getting a Meath jersey and Meath socks and togs – that was a proud moment. The county had been in the All-Ireland senior final the year before. In school I told lads that I had been called into the Meath under-15 and under-16 squads and they were blown away.

Even my aunties were all talking about their nephew Rory playing for Meath. That gave me a feeling that is hard to describe, and it became a more central part of my life. It's impossible to fully appreciate how much the GAA has done in keeping young lads from going off the rails. I don't know if people always understand that. The GAA comes in for a lot of criticism at times and the positive benefits it has on society is something most of us can't even see or will never fully know.

Realising that I was a fairly good footballer encouraged me to train more. It made me feel better about myself. Suddenly I had a purpose. Football became my addiction. The troubles I had in school were still there but my final years doing the LCA were a help in restoring some of the confidence I had lost along the way. Football did me the world of good during those years. I loved exercise because of that endorphin rush it gave me. In hindsight it was my medication.

Chapter 4

Club and county

The year I was born Meath won the All-Ireland for the first time in 20 years and remained a force in football for the next decade, with Sean Boylan in charge of a cast of outstanding footballers. I didn't attend the 1996 All-Ireland final when Meath defeated Mayo in a hot-tempered replay, the winning point coming from Brendan Reilly, who would later manage us in Donaghmore-Ashbourne for a few years. But I can remember the Sam Maguire being paraded through Ashbourne afterwards. You don't forget moments like that.

It all began when, as a young lad, I followed my sister Carol up to the 'back field', as it was known, behind St Declan's Primary School. That's where my passion took root, in the acorn academies for kids getting a first taste of Gaelic games. Whenever I was feeling low in school, the Gaelic football team was my refuge, a place where I felt that I was somebody. And because I was so much taller than my teammates I tended to be noticed and have a telling influence on the field, being strong under a high ball, good enough to eventually play minor and under-21 for my county.

As a teenager I attended the 2001 All-Ireland football final, the last time Meath appeared in one, when Galway's Padraic Joyce gave us an unmerciful going-over. It shows you how quickly your luck can turn. I was at the semi-final a few weeks before where Meath absolutely hammered Kerry. It was very strange singing 'cheerio, cheerio' to stunned Kerry supporters as they left the stadium. And there's me, only 14, and the neck on me slagging all these Kerry followers who had seen it all many times over. Leaving Croke Park that evening everyone in Meath thought we'd the All-Ireland in the bag. I went along with a mixed group of Ashbourne lads, some in their late teens, so there were cans of beer being passed around in anticipation of a toast to a famous Meath victory. At 14 I was over six feet, so I looked drinking age.

We were in the Nally Stand for the final and my only memory of it is Joyce putting the ball over the bar and then doing it again and again and again. And I kept thinking to myself, *Who is marking this fella?* For a while it was Darren Fay, one of the best full backs ever, but no matter who went on him that day Joyce was unmarkable. In my mind's eye I see this relentless stream of Galway scores. I remember meeting Joyce years later and telling him how that day he had broken my heart. That was sport in a nutshell. Up one week, down the next – just like life. And like the Frank Sinatra line, I could be riding high in April, shot down in May.

Some years earlier Trevor Giles and Nigel Nestor brought the Sam Maguire cup to St Declan's and I was in awe of these special guests, especially Trevor, in the reverential way you would look at county players at that age. Those Meath footballers filled your head with dreams of following in their footsteps and playing in Croke Park.

My own age group in Donaghmore-Ashbourne never won anything, but I did have some success playing with the team a year up. At the age of 12, I won an under-13 league medal and another at under-15. Like most players, you remember your first win. I'll never forget coming home through the village after winning the under-13 league and blaring the horns and waving the flags. There I was with my head out my father's car window, no safety belt on, waving a Donaghmore-Ashbourne flag at randomers going about their business in the middle of the day.

Football in my teenage years earned me a status I was nowhere near attaining elsewhere. Getting on the Meath under-15 team started a journey that led on to me captaining the Meath minors in 2005. The same year I was captain of the Meath Vocational Schools team, captain of the Donaghmore-Ashbourne minors, and captain of my Ashbourne secondary school team. None of the teams won anything and the following year all those teams landed Leinster titles. You could say I wasn't a lucky captain! Yet playing was the drug. Being made captain, being given that trust and responsibility, was a massive boost to my self-confidence.

As was, of course, playing for the county. I was called into the Meath minor panel by Benny Reddy in 2003. Dublin knocked out Meath in the first round and Laois went on to win the All-Ireland. We went down to Stradbally to play Laois in the Leinster League at the end of the January, 2004, and although we had a strong enough team, they had a lot of really good footballers, some with the experience of winning an All-Ireland. Brendan Quigley was midfield, and I ended up marking him, Craig Rogers was there, as was Cahir Healy. And we beat them and controlled much of the game. We left Stradbally that day thinking we were going to win the All-Ireland.

I got the biggest eye-opener of my football career when Laois came to Navan in the Leinster minor championship on a boiling hot day in the middle of May 2004. I don't know why but we were given long-sleeved jerseys by the county board to wear on a day when the temperature was in the high twenties. We were all pumped up, running over and back, hitting each other and saying that we were going to hammer these lads.

And the minute the ball was thrown in, Laois made mincemeat of us. I didn't start that game but came off the bench after 20 minutes. Everyone was panicking. We were demolished. Sean Dempsey, Laois manager that day, was a cute hoor. Turns out he ran the hole out of them either that morning or the night before we played them in Stradbally, or so I was told.

That was a big day for me, my first championship appearance for the county minor team, at still only 17 years of age. But I wasn't fooling myself: it's easy coming into a game looking good when your team's being hammered. The opposition has stepped off the gas a little – I just went in and caught a couple of kick-outs, muscled into them; then people say I should have started. There were a lot of club people there from Ashbourne supporting me and it was an honour to have made the team, but the result dampened the day.

For the following year, 2005, my final season as a Meath minor, we had Dudley Farrell at the helm, assisted by Sean Kelly and Sean Barry, who would have gone to manage my club, two great football men. A small nucleus of players were still eligible from the previous year, the likes of myself, Willie Milner, Chris Carney, Shane Monaghan and Davey Reynolds. The early-year signals were positive. We were going well and I was playing really good football and had made the midfield position my own. One of my proudest moments was when we played against Cavan in our last friendly before the championship and they announced that I would be captaining the team. When Dudley broke the news there was a round of applause. We ran out on the pitch for that game and I was on cloud nine.

This was a noteworthy landmark for our club because usually players from Donaghmore-Ashbourne don't captain Meath county teams. It was rare enough for them to play county, let alone be captain. I couldn't wait until I got back home to tell club stalwart Christy Tormey (Lord rest him), Emma Tormey, his daughter, and Gerry Delaney, all these lynchpin figures. And the likes of Sean Harmon and Rory Maguire would have played Meath minor a few years before me. I'll always hold Dudley in high regard for that. We weren't a traditional club; we weren't a Skryne, we weren't a Navan O'Mahonys. But he put his faith in me. He was willing to take a risk.

We were up against Kildare in the first match of the 2005 Leinster minor championship in Navan. I didn't play well. In a way it got to me: the occasion, the captaincy, the weight of expectation. Like, I remember the morning of the game getting all hyped up and imagining all these Kildare lads I was going to get wired into. And now there was additional pressure. I was considered one of the main players.

It's gas the things that go through your head in a match, but I was thinking at one stage during the play that I'd let the whole club down. My man might have won a ball and kicked it over the bar and I am running back to my position thinking of all the club people in the stand supporting me and how I'm failing them. Self-doubt spreads like wildfire and your confidence goes up in smoke. And yet we won. And we beat a Kildare team that was fancied.

Beating Kildare meant we had reached the Leinster semi-finals, the gateway to Croke Park. We faced Offaly in Mullingar. I had a much better game and dominated the midfield area. But we lost to the last kick of the game, courtesy of Rory Connor, who was marking me, a son of Richie Connor and a distant relation. I know Rory well. And I always say that I marked him for the whole game and then the cute hoor got on the end of a move and kicked it over the bar. And that was it. We lost. Beaten by a point.

That was a horrible defeat to take. Had we won, I was
going to be playing in Croke Park, captaining Meath
on Leinster final day as an 18-year-old. That would have
been the ultimate dream come true. It was a Dublin–Laois
Leinster senior final so a lot of people in Ashbourne who
support Dublin would have been going to it. And for me to
be able to lead out Meath would have been the perfect day.
When the dust settled, that's what killed me.

Joe Gibney used to call me into his office at Ashbourne
Community School to discuss games. He didn't spare me
after my poor performance against Kildare. Though a
straight talker, Joe was a good soul with a good heart. When
I was made Meath minor captain he made sure there was a
picture of me put up in the school to mark the achievement.
He made a bit of a fuss over it, which was really kind and
thoughtful of him, something I'll always appreciate.

After minor, there was the county under-21s. Eamonn
Barry and Benny Reddy invited me in and we played Cavan
in a friendly where they tried me out at full forward. It
was one of those days when I could do nothing wrong and
everything I touched turned to gold. I contributed 2–2 from
play, as well as setting up other scores – and they weren't
even dirty, 'farmery' goals. Caught a ball, turned, back of
the net. Out in front, turned, back of the net. And then
two points from play – one off either foot. The fella I was
marking said, 'Fucking hell, how come you're not on the
Meath senior panel?' I said, 'I'm only 18.' He goes,' Oh my
god.'

All my friends from my club were going, 'What the fuck was that?' They knew I hadn't that in me. I came off the pitch and Eamonn Barry, who was the Meath senior manager at the time too, said, 'Rory, I never knew you were a full forward.'

'Neither did I!' I replied.

Benny persisted with me at full forward for maybe the next three games and I might have scored a point in total. And that was the end of that.

We played against Kildare, who had already knocked out Dublin, in the 2006 Leinster under-21 championship. I came on with 20 minutes to go in the middle of the field. Again, a bit like the Laois minor game, they were much better than us, winning by eight points. In 2007 we lost a Leinster under-21 semi-final to Offaly in Tullamore, I still can't figure out how. In my final year as a county under-21 in 2008, Colm Coyle was over the team and we trained with the seniors. We played Kildare and we got trounced, 1–14 to 0–4, before the end of February. Way off the pace. Eoin Reilly, David Morgan and myself were all playing – a mark of the club's progress but a disappointing day for Meath.

The most honest football critics were local, the ones who knew you inside out. Christy Tormey was unflinching. You rarely got a compliment off Christy. Like the day we played against Edenderry in the Leinster intermediate club semi-final in 2007 and I had a stormer. I met Christy in the smoking area of a pub on the way home. He took his fag out, tapped it on the box, looked at me and said, 'It's about time you took off those red fucking gloves,' and walked away.

I wore red gloves in the county intermediate final and didn't play that well. And I'd no gloves on against Edenderry and played out of my skin. I walked away thinking, *That's the best compliment I've ever got.* It was as good as 20 people saying you'd a man-of-the-match performance. Like, it's hard to describe Christy and do him justice. You have the committee meeting room in the club named after him. He *was* the club.

The club meant the world to me and I have the marks to prove it. When I was on my year away in Australia, Emma and I headed up the Gold Coast, with Carol and her husband Bren, for a week's break. One night we got talking about tattoos. I said that they weren't my thing but if I was ever going to get one it would be the Donaghmore-Ashbourne GAA crest. Bren said he'd choose the Leinster rugby crest. He's a big Leinster fan. And I was, 'Sure fuck it we'll get it done, will we?' And he was, 'Ah yeah, why wouldn't we. We'll get it done tomorrow.'

Anyway, we went on the beer. I got up the next day and went straight to the parlour and got the job done. And I went back to Bren and said, 'Well, when are you getting yours done?' He's like, 'I was only messing. You mad thing. Is that real?'

I don't regret getting it because I love the club but after I came back I remember we were in the showers after training and Martin Lynch, who I would have soldiered with for years, a fantastic footballer and a really good lad, says, 'Jaysus Rory, they're after spelling Donaghmore wrong!' I ran out to the mirror to check. Thankfully, Martin was only winding me up.

We are traditionally a football club but I played a bit of hurling too. The likes of Davy Gaughan and Pat Daly are still driving on the hurling in the club. Every club needs great people like that. If nothing else the hurling enabled me play out some roles in the videos I would make years later. My memories are of heavy beatings and plenty of rows. I played full back, fancied myself as a bit of a Diarmuid O'Sullivan figure. I loved hitting shoulders, coming through the middle and planting some lad. Winning a ball and driving it as far as I could, I got a great buzz out of that. I was never wristy, but I was big and strong.

One day we were playing a match up in my old school and Ciaran Finn was corner back. There was a lot of congestion in the full-back line. John Mooney, our mentor from Kilkenny, said, 'Rory! Get in there!' So I went in, threw me arse about and started swinging like fuck. Eventually I picked up the ball and cleared it and I turned around and Ciaran was laid out on the ground. I went and grabbed my man by the throat and he began to plead, 'Rory, you done that!' Apparently when I was swinging I caught Ciaran clean on the back of the head. Later we were told if he hadn't a helmet on he would've been stone dead.

I loved going into the mix, horsing lads out of it, but I stopped hurling at around 17 or 18. I didn't play any adult hurling really. We used to go and hurl the likes of Kiltale, Kildalkey, Kilmesssan and they'd beat the shit out of us. Proper hurling clubs.

And often I'd have to puck the ball out as well because the goalie might have a shite puck-out. So I'd be flat out pucking the ball out for the whole game. I might be competing with a lively lad who might be skinning me, and, at my wit's end, I'd pull on his shin, or pull somewhere, and just get the line.

But do you know what? I don't know if we ever won a game.

Football was a different matter. In 2006 we reached the quarter finals of the intermediate championship, beaten by eventual winners Rathkenny under Gerry Flanagan, which was regarded as progress. And then Andy McEntee came in and everything moved up a notch. Since then he has gone on to greater things, winning an All-Ireland club title with Ballyboden and currently managing the Meath county team. He was a different level to anything I had seen before. He started demanding standards that we weren't used to. I can't say enough good things about the man. He taught us more than just football. He taught me a lot about life. When I opened up about my depression the first person I met with was Andy.

He's easily in the top five people I have most respect for and if there was anything he could do for you he would do it. He is also the thickest fucker I ever met in my life, I had some rows with him, maybe over not starting me or whatever but once the dust settled I still don't believe there is a man more passionate about the GAA and Meath than Andy McEntee. That's all he cared about. He used to call players nearly every day, asking what you were eating or doing. I never experienced that professionalism before. I knew he was destined to be the county manager. He had too much drive not to be.

I struggled with weight and he'd always be on to me about my diet and what I was eating. As you can imagine I hate the sight of the weighing scales. One year in January, at the start of pre-season training, Andy decided all the players needed to be weighed. Because the weather was cold all the lads had plenty layers on but I was down to my boxers, trying to save on every ounce. I remember standing on the scales and looking down nervously. Andy stared the scales, which clocked around 17 and half stone, then looked up at me with a scowl. 'What the fuck is that?'

'Ah Andy, I've been in the gym a lot last few weeks.'

'You're a fat cunt, get off that scale!'

And then the following day he'd ring me. 'Rory, you know I simply can't have you at over 17 stone. Running up and down that pitch – it's not fucking possible. You need to lose weight or I'm going to have to drop you.'

'Andy, I'm trying my best!'

'You're not trying hard enough!' And then he'd send me on another diet. But the truth of the matter was, I just ate too much.

I tried to stick to it but living at home, with my mother's cooking, it was a tough ask. She used to make big portions, so what would happen is I'd only eat half the stew, trying to be weight-conscious, and then I'd go back later and eat the other half. And then I'd probably get sick at training. I didn't eat badly – I just ate too much.

In another life I'd probably play rugby because I had that physique. I was always too big. If I as much as looked at a bench press I'd put on muscle. But running was torture. I trained by myself to ensure I was not too far off the pace when group training started in pre-season and I'd still be near the back. Long-distance running killed me. Doing laps of the field was hell.

But Andy understood me and he always got 100 per cent out of me. I think he knew I was – I have no problem saying it – one of the most dedicated people around. I wanted to win with the club. I often ratted lads who were drinking to him because I wanted us to win. At the time you were known as the rat but now people would say, 'Rory, you were dead right. We needed that. We needed a bit of discipline.' And I think McEntee saw that in me. I was limited when I got to adult football: I could catch a few balls, break a few balls, make a tackle, that was it. I never had the potential, I believe anyway, to be a senior county player. I just didn't have that football in me. But I was a handful around midfield and Andy knew that and there were lots of games I wasn't winning any ball and he could have taken me off but he'd often leave me there. He was probably too loyal to some lads.

Andy was one of those managers you wanted to please. If you went back to Kelly's pub after a match and you'd played well Andy would call you over, put out his hand and he'd squeeze and give you a look. It was like a sergeant telling his troops they'd done well. Anyone from our club to Ballyboden to the Meath minors, who he also managed, to the Meath seniors would tell you the same. There's nothing more terrifying than your phone ringing on a Monday morning after a championship loss and it's Andy McEntee. Everyone feared that phone call. Darragh Nelson of Ballyboden said the same, that it would put the fear into you.

After he first arrived we had a team meeting in Kelly's. I'd never heard of Andy McEntee up until then, though he came from a famous Nobber football family. I'd heard of Gerry McEntee, his brother, who'd won All-Irelands. But Andy, also a county player but less well known, was a mystery to me.

One day, Barry Waters, who won a senior championship with Dunboyne and who worked with me at the time, called me over. 'I heard you got Andy McEntee? You'd better brace yourselves. We called him Andy Smackentee in Dunboyne. This lad is a headbanger. I tell you – you'll be fit now, Rory.'

He asked at that first meeting what our ambitions were. And big dopey Rory puts up his hand and says, 'I'd like to win an intermediate championship in the next three years.' I was only being honest. And he just gave me a look as much to say: *What kind of ambition is that? Why would you wait three years?*

The day after I lost a Leinster semi-final with the Meath under-21s the club had a league game and I told Andy I'd play, but I went on the beer and didn't show up. At training on the Tuesday night he came up to me and said:

'Listen, I don't give a fuck what county panel you're on. If you've any ambition to play midfield in this club you need to be here and you need to be training. I have Ian Dowd, I have Eoin Reilly, I've enough lads, I don't need you. If you want to be here, I need you. If you don't want to be here, fuck off.'

And I was: *who is this fella?* He just laid down the law. And from that day, and that kick in the hole, I started working hard and did everything he told me to.

The McEntees have this look in their eyes that only people who know the McEntees will know what I'm talking about. Gerry and Andy in particular. And in fairness, Larry and Tony, the other brothers, they have it. I call it the McEntee look. It's a cold, dead-eyed expression. And if you get that look it's not good. And that's the look Andy will give you when he is sending instructions to the pitch.

One time Colm O Méalóid gave a ball away. And Andy goes, 'Colm! Colm!' And Colm made some kind of dismissive hand gesture. Andy was not impressed. 'Colm! Don't give me the fucking hand! Look at me, Colm!' He was half mad, like. But I can't thank the man enough. I took more from him than football, I learned a lot about life.

He had this thing after matches, where he might start off saying, 'I'm going to say a few things and I don't give a fuck.'

And whenever he said those words you knew he was going to lay down the law. He didn't pull punches. He just wanted to win. He was a winner.

At times you thought Andy was a bit of a psycho but he was probably what we needed. He got results. We were an intermediate club team and he was ringing lads flat out every day about how to improve. He had to change the mentality and the culture. He had this thing in his head that I couldn't kick a ball. When I caught a kick-out I had to lay it off. So I kicked less. But I listened to him and did what he asked.

We had some great nights together. I loved going on the beer with him. In 2008 when he wanted to win the senior title in the first year up he called a half dozen of us together, myself, Niall Farrell, Eoin Reilly, Cormac McGill, Dave Morgan and Colm O Méalóid, who he viewed as leaders, and arranged that we all gather one day in Dublin for a meeting. He chose a Thai restaurant off Grafton Street. We were only young lads. I called in sick to work that day in order to be present. I felt I had no other option.

We all arrived at the venue. Andy says, 'Anybody want any wine, what wine do you drink?'

I said, 'I don't know, Andy, I've never really had wine.'

We had loads of wine.

He starts talking about wanting leaders in his team, and how he was looking at us lads to drive it. Standard stuff really, standard now but not standard then. McEntee was ahead of the time. 'I want you to lead, lads, on and off the pitch.'

We had the serious football talk for an hour and then it just became a drinking session. We went into Kehoe's, McEntee's credit card behind the bar and pints galore. And with McEntee he'd often fall asleep when he'd a few pints in him but he'd be still listening, so say if you mentioned a player, he'd lift his head up and go, 'I hate that fucking cunt!' and then put the head back down again.

And then all of a sudden he announced 'Right! I'm going home.'

'Where're you going Andy?' we all asked.

'Catherine's picking me up. Dunboyne AGM is on tonight and I'm gonna go tell a few people what I really think of them.'

We all said, 'Andy, telling you now, don't go.'

That was where he lived, Dunboyne. I had this vision of a club AGM where he comes in baloobas drunk with wine and Guinness, slating the whole committee. He'd be liable to do that.

Then he rings me the next day. 'Hello Rory, how are you?'

'Ah … dying a bit.'

'Yeah, good oul fun. Come here, what the fuck is bourbon?'

'I don't actually know, Andy.'

'Well some cunt was drinking bourbon on my fucking credit card. There's a big bill, I want to know who it is.'

'Well Colm was late to the party so he went straight on the whiskey.'

'Ah no that's fair enough, Colm was catching up. But there's a load of bourbons here and someone was piggybacking on my credit card.'

I can't say enough about Andy McEntee. I often think when facing a tough situation – it could be on stage or wherever – *What would Andy do?* And Andy generally doesn't give a fuck. But he had great morals. He was a loose cannon but his heart was in the right place. He loves football and he loves winning. I don't think we gave enough; we should have won a senior championship. Andy went into Ballyboden and told them they were going to win the All-Ireland. And they fairly laughed at him.

I was drinking in a bar in Edinburgh watching Ballyboden win the All-Ireland club title in 2016, with Andy in charge, and I was so happy for him. I really was. The final whistle went and had I been there, I would have given him a hug, I know how much work he put into that.

We beat Castletown in the county intermediate final in 2007. We were red-hot favourites but they were a hardy, seasoned team. Niall Farrell, the best I've played with and a cousin of Peter Canavan, scored nine points. But some days he wasn't interested and he might as well be sitting at home drinking tea and watching the telly. He got a score when we badly needed one. I wasn't winning much ball, and he said, 'Stay down, Rory.' And he leapt over my head, caught the ball, whizzed in and out between six lads and put it over the bar. To me that was grabbing the game by the scruff of the neck.

At half time during the 2007 county final, Andy hit all the right notes. He spoke of it not being about medals or celebration but something more lasting; about seeing

someone in years to come where you'll nod at each and know
that you once won a championship with that man. And
there are lads I have fallen out of contact with, but when I
do meet them we both know, like Andy said. When we won
the intermediate title he got us into a huddle afterwards and
said that these days don't come round often. 'Look around
you, this is special. I'd advise you not to drink too much
tonight. Embrace it.'

Now I don't think any of us listened to his advice, to be
honest with you, but one of the memorable moments was
having a quiet pint outside Ashbourne House later that day
with all the players, reflecting on the year and where it had
taken us.

That evening we were paraded on a truck down through
the Main Street and began a wild week of celebrations
including two visits to Copper's. But the stand-out moment
came on the Monday when I was one of the players who
brought the cup to St Declan's on a tour of the schools.
Frank Reidy, the principal, said, 'Oh, we have Rory here
now, who played midfield yesterday. Did anyone see Rory?'
Big cheer.

That was a lovely moment: to be able to say that, even if I
did nothing else with my life, at least I helped Donaghmore-
Ashbourne win a county championship they hadn't won in
50 years.

Winning that county title, even though it was intermediate, was a proud moment. Like Andy told us, it will be
there for the rest of time.

Chapter 5

Emma

I left school in 2005, having completed the Leaving Cert Applied exam and captained the Meath minors. Where to now? Tony had left school after third year and was already working. Austin had also left. While I made it to the finishing line, I was no clearer about what I wanted to do when I stepped out into the world looking for work. There were no real options that I could see.

There were others like me, not remotely academic, lost in the same fog, craving direction. I knew Willie Milner from Summerhill through playing on the same underage teams with Meath. Willie is a gas ticket and, like me, had no interest in school and also ended up doing the Leaving Cert Applied. We both decided to apply for a sports and recreational management course in Coláiste Íde in Finglas. I looked on it as something to keep the mother off my back. I wasn't short on company, with Philly McMahon in the same class and a number of people I knew from Ashbourne. Linda Mullen was a good childhood friend of mine, she came from Castle Crescent, and Danielle Mongan and

Shane Whelan were also locals, so we all car-pooled. It was a great experience and I enjoyed it. But it proved a dead end.

After six months I waved the white flag. I loved the practical side of the course, but once they veered into physiology and anatomy, the theory end, I felt lost. It was like being back in school again. The experience was not in vain, however, because it was there that I first met Emma, my future wife.

I didn't go there to find a wife, obviously, and I'm fairly sure she didn't choose the course with the intention of landing a husband. But that's what happened. Our paths crossed and we never looked back. Emma was part of a group of maybe five or six from the Blanchardstown area on the same course and they stuck together, all good-looking girls. You could tell the difference between a girl from Ashbourne and a girl from Blanchardstown by how they dressed. The Dublin girls were a bit ahead in the fashion stakes.

It wasn't that Emma completely stood out from the crowd, but instinctively I felt there was something about her. She was extremely shy; I was the complete opposite. I think I went up to her and said, 'Hey, my name is Rory' and she froze on the spot. I got her number and sent her a text and we began texting each other back and forth. In those Nokia 3210 days there was no WhatsApp or Snapchat, just basic texting.

One day I texted her and she never replied. A few days passed. Nothing. I was over in Tony's house, ranting to his mother, Theresa, saying how I liked this one, and the neck of her not texting me back. I was a kind of cocky fella then and I thought she should have responded. Then three or four days later I got a text off her saying, 'Hey Rory, sorry I never texted back, we were playing a match in Erin's Isle with the ladies' team and my phone and my bag got robbed.'

Emma was big into the GAA as well. She played for the Dublin minors and Castleknock at the time and that helped us establish a connection. We even went for kick-arounds together. She was extremely fast and mobile, everything I wasn't, a very slick kind of player. But then like a lot of women she stopped playing in her late teens, which was a pity. I tried to coax her to play with Donaghmore-Ashbourne but she never got back into it. Even now when we go for a kick-around she is still well able to play.

Coláiste Íde is known as a soccer college, although they played Gaelic football too and while I was there we won an All-Ireland colleges title, with Philly on the same team. But soccer was more prevalent and there was a soccer clique that sat together in the canteen. Emma told me that one lad from that group had been repeatedly texting her, though she said she wasn't interested. Undeterred, he continued to send her messages. I asked her to identify him for me. She brushed it off, told me to ignore him, but I managed to establish who the stalker was.

I decided to confront him. But first I turned to Philly and Willie for back-up. Willie would have been six foot, not as big as me but a better footballer. Two good feet. Bundles of talent. And if there was a fight Willie would be there for you.

And sure Philly, as the future showed, wasn't the kind to shy away from a row. I asked the two lads, 'Will you get my back here if something sparks off?' They nodded.

I walked up to this guy with Philly and Willie behind me and I just said, 'Hey what's your name?'

He gave his name and I said, 'Listen, will you stop texting Emma Bates, you're wrecking her head.'

'I'm not texting her,' he said.

I said, 'Listen, stop texting her or I'll pull the head off you. Do you understand?'

I knew he was never going to ask me outside with the two boys standing behind me and I was a rough-looking diamond too. And that was the end of that.

The relationship quickly blossomed. I started at Coláiste Íde in September and we started going out in November – the 27th, she reminds me enough times. Fifteen years later, we're still together.

Emma is the original reason why I believe in following your gut feeling. There was something telling me to keep at her. It was also my first proper relationship. I knew she was the one, yet I was kind of half-raging that it had come this soon, thinking, *I'm only 18 and I'm stuck with this one.* But I kinda knew that it was meant to be.

Peter and Mary are Emma's parents, and when I met her, Shauna, her sister, was only 14 and like a little sister to me. Shauna has a young child now, called Clayton-Cole, and she's engaged to Jay, who I'd be very fond of. Peter at the start was a bit cold. I suppose he was looking out for his daughter,

like any father would. I was six foot four and a raving Meath
man. *Like, who is this fella?* he must have thought. But we
get on like a house on fire now. I just had to earn his trust.
I'd be doing the same with my daughter. Peter is originally
from Ballyfermot and Mary is from Manor Street in the
heart of town. True blue Dubs and they've given me plenty
of slagging in recent years with Dublin winning all those
All-Irelands.

Mary's mother Lily, a lovely woman whom we all
adored and who took a good shine to me, passed away on
the Wednesday after Donaghmore-Ashbourne won the
intermediate championship in 2007. Emma and I were with
her, and I saw her take her last breath. I had been on the
highest of highs after winning the championship only a few
days before. I remember walking outside after she'd passed
away and bawling my eyes out. Mary and Peter were abroad
at the time and had to fly home. It was so difficult, talking
to them on the phone.

Mary was an only child so that would have been hard for
her, with her father already gone. I held it together as best I
could for Emma but once I left Lily's room that Wednesday
I fell asunder. I was only 20 at the time. And people who
drink a lot, as I had done in the days after the county final,
will know that three days on the beer plays havoc with your
emotions and nerves.

A lot would change in my life by the time I married
Emma in 2017. We had our first child, Ella, in 2012, and
Zach followed in 2018. Even though Emma and I are very

different personalities, we have so much in common. She wouldn't dream of being in a video although I persuaded her to make an exception when she appeared in one earlier this year. I know she won't be making a habit of it. She keeps her social media private. She gets lot of follower requests on Instagram and places like that, but she's not into that. That is what I like about her as well.

She is also patient and accommodating. We were going to the cinema one time and I asked her what she'd like to see. 'I don't mind,' she replied, as she usually does. I was mad to see *Saw*, which is a violent horror film about a robot who goes around chopping up people. She went along and it was only later I discovered that she's terrified of horror films. Yet she sat through *Saw* and never said a word.

She's very picky with food, a disaster. Again, we're poles apart in that respect. My mam was feeding me two bowls of porridge every morning, probably from the age of three. She had me on solids after seven or eight weeks. I have a stupidly big appetite. Comes from my dad. By the time my mother would have served the dinner my father would be putting on the kettle, the dinner gone, and I'd be looking at him. We'd both be savages for food. I eat Emma's sides when we're out. The appetite is fairly ferocious.

We stayed together through all the hard times, when money was scarce and I was going through my own battles with gambling and a lack of career direction. She lived with my hyper moods. I'd say regarding rows we were probably as good as you'd get in a relationship. She keeps me in line a lot. Without her I don't think I'd be who I am. I have a good heart but I'd be wild and easily blown off course. I do believe the saying that behind every good man there's a good woman. I really do. She keeps everything together. She'd tell me to calm down or cop the fuck on if we're out on a night and I'm getting to be a bit of a eejit. And I think that's important in a relationship, having that bit of an understanding. Now she drives me mad at times and I drive her, as you can imagine, madder still. But that's part and parcel of a relationship.

While Emma stayed with the course in Coláiste Íde, I had to look elsewhere. My dad began encouraging me to master a trade. He suggesting butchering, which I had no interest in whatsoever. I might have had the big hands of a butcher, but the thought of it, butchering cows and pigs? Fuck that. I never put on the apron.

I knew it wasn't butchering, but what then? I hadn't a notion. You would think that by the time you reached 18, after all those school years, you would have a fair idea of what you were good at. I had no interest in solving equations. I hated the sight of a jigsaw. I hated the sight of a crossword. But there's people that love that. Let them power on. And let those more hands-on do what suits them. My biggest gift is being a people person, talking to people and bringing others into conversations. That's what I needed to focus on. But I had to find that out for myself. My dad wanted me to take up a trade, so I went in as an apprentice electrician.

I can't begin to explain how unsuited I was to this. I told Tony and he actually burst out laughing. 'You! An electrician, the big fucking hands on you and the dopey head on you?'

'I know, Tony, just keeping the dad happy, you know yourself.'

Mick Beggy was a legendary full back in the local GAA club. He was also a manager in a local electrical equipment supplier company, BMC Manufacturing, where I started as a first-year apprentice on a four-year journey.

I was like a fish out of water. One day Mick said, 'Rory, go and do us 20 distribution board labels.' And I spent forever making up these labels to make sure they were near to perfection. I really wanted to impress him.

'Job complete,' I went, 'there you are, Mick.'

And he looks at them, and says, 'Rory, how do you spell distribution?'

I had to go and do the labels all over again. Mick would have known me well. He would have had a lot of lads through his hands. I would say he knew there was no hope of me becoming an electrician. I did nothing to persuade him otherwise. Even when we were drilling labels onto a panel, the harder I tried the more crooked it would be. And that went back to my confidence. I had no confidence whatsoever and if anyone looked at me, I would drop the screw or whatever.

But I got through that first year and Mick sent me to FÁS in Finglas, the next step, and I actually had great craic because it was full of characters. Luckily enough I'm a Jack the Lad so I can handle banter. All these lads were wiring cookers and immersions and I was wondering what is an earth wire and what is a live wire and what is a neutral. What are they talking about? But I didn't tell anyone. Again, I didn't want anyone to think I was stupid, because if I was to go into the room and say, 'Sorry, can someone explain to me what a neutral wire is?' they'd say, 'Who the fuck let this weapon in here?'

Now, there were a few sound lads on the FÁS segment who would come up, and say, 'Rory, just fix that there.' They were what you'd call the good people in life. They could have made a show of me, but they didn't. It's people like that who keep you going in life. Kind-hearted people.

But mostly it was torture. When we were filling out the FÁS forms I had to ask a friend of mine, Sean Benville, who did the apprenticeship with me, how to spell 'electrician'. I knew I should have jumped ship then but I said, fuck it, it was all to keep the oul lad happy, to keep him off my back.

See, you got paid in FÁS every week once you showed up and clocked in, and I was just showing up. I was meant to be learning but when the rest of them were all powering on, I was just drawing pictures on my copybook. I was gone, my mind was elsewhere. I saw out the last three months because I was getting paid for it. The minute I came back to BMC I knew it. I was gone.

Mick called me in.

'Well, Rory, how did you get on in FÁS?'

'Ah yeah, Mick, bit of craic, you know yourself.'

'Well, your results are back. There's eight modules and you passed one.'

'I'm actually happy enough with the one, Mick, what was that?'

'It was your attendance, Rory.'

'Ah yeah, ah sure you know yourself, Mick.'

And Mick, being a friend, said, 'You're a good fella, I don't want to sack you, but I don't want to see you on Monday morning, do you understand?'

And I said, 'One hundred per cent, Mick, no bother.' And that was my electrician's journey over.

To me that ending made perfect sense, but I had to tell my dad. See, my dad, being good with his hands, couldn't understand how his son was so hopeless at these tasks. In woodwork in school I was the worst in the class. If everyone else was a millimetre off, I was an inch away. And Joe O'Connor couldn't understand that. Like, I couldn't change a tyre if my life depended on it. Even now, OK, I'd do it, but it could take an hour.

That time spent trying to become an electrician lasted about a year, all told. I learned nothing except that I was no electrician. One of the apprentices who had a kind heart called me over at one point during my ordeal, noticed I was in bother. He took sympathy, tried an intervention.

'Look', he said supportively, 'I was where you are at one stage.' And, with the patience of a saint, he'd take me through it. 'This, Rory, is the panel.'

He'd talk to me for 15 minutes and I'd take nothing from that conversation. Might as well have been speaking Swahili. I was catapulted back to those schooldays, with the goldfish attention span. I had no interest in what was inside a panel. If he'd said, 'Rory, pick your starting 15 there for Meath,' I would have said, 'Hey, I'll do that.'

I just couldn't see what I would end up doing. I was lost. During those uncertain days, I'd ask myself, *Well, what is for you, Rory? You left the college course. Left the electrician's apprenticeship.* You start asking yourself questions you have no answer for. And it's a dark place. I wish someone had said to me, *Listen Rory, you'll be OK, just hang in there.* I would have to search alone, with no map. I couldn't see myself owning a house, a car, the normal things, because I just couldn't do what you get paid to do. I'd never be on good money and hold a conventional job.

At BMC, because a lot of the lads there were into it, betting made me feel that bit more normal. It became part of the week. Playing poker was big as well, we'd play in different houses. Much of it was out of sheer boredom, because when we weren't drinking due to the football we turned to betting to spend our money, the idea being that if I can't go out I'll spend that €50 in the bookies. That's the kind of attitude we had. We were looking for an adrenaline kick, really.

I had a dream of owning my own construction company but then I'd cop myself on, give myself a reality check: *Rory, you need to be good at construction to own a construction company.* I kept my thoughts to myself. Nobody spoke about stuff like that at the time, we bottled it all up. *Ah Rory, you know what, a kick up the hole is all you need.* After all, teachers in school told me I'd amount to nothing. And I was starting to believe them.

Chapter 6

Dead end

By hook or by crook I got a job over in Eastpoint Industrial Estate, working in a call centre for Bord Gáis. That lasted three months. I had to get the bus into town and then the Luas out to this place. I think my salary was around €18,000 a year. It was horrible, leaving Ashbourne at 7 a.m. and getting home at 7 p.m. The only thing that kept me going for those three months was that it was during the period when Donaghmore-Ashbourne were winning the intermediate championship. We won it in October 2007 and then we went on a run to the Leinster final where our near neighbours, Fingal Ravens, beat us in Parnell Park. For a while, during this extended championship win, I was going into the job hungover to shreds on a Monday morning. And I'd say, 'No, you don't understand, this doesn't happen all the time, we're on a Leinster run here.' Sure they knew nothing about the GAA. I just spent my time in that job emailing lads off the team – many had proper jobs and had gone to college. I didn't answer half the calls that came through, I hung up on most of them.

I worked with some nice people but the wages were terrible and I knew deep down it was leading me nowhere. When I was sitting there in the call centre, negative thoughts had a field day. *Rory, every teacher was right about you, pal. You're useless.* I knew the job was only a stopgap and that I could be released at any time. And I'd say that unless you were drunk or took a knife to the interviewer, you would have got that job. After three months I left. Another dead end. And again, back home to explain. '*Oh Mam, it was too hard. It wasn't for me.*'

Near the end of 2007 I got wind that Quinn Direct Insurance was hiring people as claims handlers. I put in the CV and, lo and behold, I got the phone call. I thought, *Jesus, they must be desperate, giving me an interview.* I got Carol to do up a CV for me, she'd some HR experience. She bumped up my sports achievements, all based on being a good team player. But sport can be both a blessing and a curse.

After losing the Leinster intermediate club final in 2007 some serious drinking started. We gave it a right lash locally on the Sunday of the game and then on the Monday we went over to socialise with the team that defeated us, Fingal Ravens, on their territory, which is only a few miles outside of Ashbourne inside the Dublin border in Rolestown. We were drinking madly with the Ravens lads till all hours and next day I had the job interview with Quinn.

Tony drove me over because he was, we'll say, less shot than I was. The interview was at 11 o'clock and I'm just after milling a breakfast roll and the mother is after eating the head off me as I'm going out the door. 'Of all the times,' she says, 'and the head on you going out that door!'

I thought I had no chance of getting this job. A woman conducted the interview. 'So, tell me about yourself,' she asked.

I gave the usual spiel: an honest fella, blah blah blah. And she said, 'Here, I see you've completed an insurance exam?'

And I was thinking, *What are you talking about?* Obviously my sister put down something on the CV to beef it up a bit. So that was a bit of a left-fielder. She asked me how I would implement something in a certain scenario. Again, no idea what she was talking about. I gave some vacant answer and she just stared at me.

And I don't know what came over me, but I just said to her out straight: 'I do apologise – I'm very hungover.'

She stared at me like I had ten heads.

I said, 'Listen I'm not sure if you're into the GAA, but my club played in the Leinster final at the weekend and unfortunately we lost and I went on the beer yesterday. I apologise, I'm not usually like this.' I was also missing half an eyebrow from a house party.

'Do you mind if I open a window? I feel bit nauseous.'

I opened the window and sat back down and I just stared at her, expecting her to say, 'OK, this interview is finished.' But she said, 'I actually am into the GAA. You might know my friend.' And she named a lad I had played against a few times.

And I thought to myself: *bingo!* And I says, 'Ah yeah, I know him well, a really nice fella.'

Anyway, we chatted about that and it turned out she was from a town not too far from Ashbourne, and we chatted a bit about that too and we didn't chat anything about Quinn Direct and by Jaysus I got a phone call the next day saying that I was hired. I couldn't believe I got the job. My mam couldn't believe it. Nor my dad. Nobody could believe it.

I tell that story about the job interview for Quinn Direct in my mental health talks. I use it to highlight the point that sometimes in life you need to be honest. If I hadn't come clean, not told her I was hungover, she would have just thought I was a write-off. It would have been curtains. But honesty and the GAA connection basically got me the job. That's the bottom line.

So I'd got the job but I didn't know what I had to do. Not a clue. Official claims handler, it stated. I went in anyway and we had to get a week's training. Six at a pod, gathered round in a circle. Gillian, my head supervisor, was there and Lisa O'Kelly, a lovely woman, would have been my regional manager, and Terry Byrne my team leader. I was handed 40 claims and I thought, *oh my god what are you doing here Rory?* Emails would be coming in, *To whom it may concern,* and I'd just delete them. Any email I didn't understand I'd delete. The only email I would respond to was where someone asked me to lunch. A lifelong friend, Brian Byrne, worked here and we used to go for lunch together. Brian has been a great support to me and still is one of the most positive people I know.

After six months of making an absolute hames of anything I touched, Lisa called me into the office.

'Rory, how do you feel you're getting on?'

'To be honest with you, Lisa, I'm struggling.'

'Thank god you said that.'

'What do you mean?'

'If you'd said you were getting on well I would have been worried about you.'

She said I had messed up numerous claims, continually closing claims the company had to reopen. I was just closing claims to beat the band because you got extra money if you closed claims – a bonus, like. So I lied: I pretended I was ringing insurance companies and putting down fake names. But they kept me on. Why? I think because she knew I had good human qualities that enabled me to hit if off well with the team. I suppose I lightened the mood in the office. I mightn't have been the best at doing the job but I can guarantee that my colleagues were in better form.

Before I started the job I'd heard of the Quinn Christmas parties, which were legendary affairs, held in the Slieve Russell, Sean Quinn's place, where it was free hotel and free bar all night. By the time of the 2009 Christmas party the economic recession was starting to really kick in. So rather than a free bar everyone had five drink vouchers. You were presented with five raffle-style tickets in an envelope and I thought to myself, if I go over to Eason's and buy a book of similar tickets then this night will be free at the bar for me.

Later I felt like Don Corleone. I was out in the smoking area at the hotel and people coming up to me saying, 'Are you the fella that has the vouchers?'

'I am indeed,' I'd say, and hand them a few.

At one stage I staggered up to the bar and said, 'Can I have a vodka and Red Bull please?'

I went to hand the girl a ticket and she says, 'We're not taking them anymore.'

I said, 'Why?'

And she goes, 'That's why.' And I looked over at the till and there were hundreds of them everywhere. They'd copped on.

Soon after this the possibility of voluntary redundancy came up. The company was struggling and laying off people. Chris Bradley, a work buddy of mine, and myself were both excited about this as we didn't like the job anyway. Everyone else was thinking of their mortgage and kids and that. Lisa O'Kelly, who I got on with very well, brought me in and said, 'Rory, there's a redundancy offer.' She quoted the figure, €11,500.

'Is that for the whole company?' I asked her.

'No that's *your* redundancy.'

'Jesus, where do I sign?'

TV3 were down covering workers, despondent and fretting over their future, leaving the plant in Blanchardstown. And here was I getting €11.5k for doing nothing in there for the last two and a half years. I even made it on the television news reports, big smiley head on me, toasting the generosity of Sean Quinn. Tony's father, Noel (also known as Scobie), said he was watching the same news report in some pub in Oldtown and this oul lad remarked: 'That's the kind of lad we want in this country, bit of happiness, be delighted with what you get instead of giving out.'

With the windfall from Quinn, Emma and I agreed to head to Australia for a year. It wasn't something I had earmarked as a priority but Emma was very keen. And I knew I was constantly holding her back. She was working for AIB in Swords at the time and when I got the money I didn't really have an excuse not to go. We were never going to get a mortgage at the time. And my sister Carol and her husband Bren were by then living in Sydney so we had a place to stay when we got over there.

We'd been to see them two years previously for a month but this would be a long stay and I'm a home bird. Still, we were committed to travelling. I'd keep checking my bank balance and see that 11 grand resting there. My god, it was unreal. Imagine that at 22 years of age. On the way we took in LA, Fiji and the gambler's paradise, Las Vegas.

When I was about 16 I went down to Galway with Tony for a weekend. And it was here it started – where I planted the first seeds of a gambling habit. On our arrival Tony got a text advising him to place a bet on a three-team accumulator, so we found a bookies just off Eyre Square. I remember going in, those first impressions: screens everywhere, the noise, bedlam. Tony went up to the counter and took out a tenner.

And I was thinking, *What are you doing putting a tenner on it? Sure that's mad!* I risked a fiver. The three teams all won and I might have got €30 back. I thought this was too good to be true.

And that's how it began before it spread like a cancer to the point where it nearly broke me 11 years later. We started off by doing a fiver accumulator every Saturday. We'd go in and pick a few teams. Now they rarely come in and everyone who gambles knows the sinking feeling when such and such a team lets you down with a last-minute goal – there're a lot of hardship stories when it comes to accumulators. I felt that these – small-stake weekend accumulators – would be my limit, but gradually you start going a bit deeper into the pocket.

Then it was on to horses. We all talked about form, in the company of friends, so that it became a normal part of everyday conversation. We'd regularly head down to the bookies in Ashbourne on a Saturday and stay there betting for an hour or two. You might take €30 and while there you'd see your fortunes fluctuate and your emotions yo-yo until eventually you'd leave without a button.

I remember Ann Newman, who worked in the Track, the local bookies, saying, as if she had seen the future: 'Lads, I'm telling ye now, ye are better off not being at this because what's a fiver now will be twenty or thirty before long.'

'Ah no,' we assured her, 'we'll be grand'.

Willie Milner would have been into the betting as well, and being from Summerhill, which is a horsey town, he would have access to tips. It was relatively harmless at the start but I became more immersed when I started working with BMC. Most of the older lads who worked there were keen gamblers. So every day there were tips circulating, and every Friday we'd get paid and go down to the Stag's Head and get a roll, and then we'd go into the bookies next door and put on a 'lucky 15'.

Then the lads in the GAA team would be talking about races and matches in terms of the odds available and what was good value or worth a punt. Cheltenham would come round every March and the talk revolved around tips. All you heard about was tips and more tips.

During the summer I'd find myself skipping down to the bookies on a Wednesday or Thursday evening, because of the late racing, and Emma would be ringing and I wouldn't answer the phone. I'd ring her back and say, 'Oh I'm just down in Tony's.'

And so the lying started.

I remember walking up the road on several occasions and actually punching myself in the head in disgust over what I'd lost. Then I'd half-tell my ma that I was in the bookies and lost money and she'd give me a loan of €30 or €40. The thing about gambling is that it creeps up on you, like ivy, and before you realise it the problem is out of hand.

By the time I went to Australia with Emma I had a gambling addiction. Not that I acknowledged it: on the second day of our journey, during our stop-off in Las Vegas, I'd say I lost $500, but the loss had no impact on me. This was Vegas, after all – you have to be prepared to lose. They pump air into the casinos to help you stay awake for longer. They want to keep you playing as long as possible. One night we drank the heads off ourselves and went to bed at all hours of the morning. I woke up not knowing my arse from my elbow. I told Emma I needed a coffee and asked if she wanted anything. She asked for tea. So I picked up my jeans and found around $160-worth of chips in the pockets I didn't realise I'd won the night before. It was maybe 10.30 a.m. I was heading towards the coffee dock when I spotted a roulette table. I thought of the $160. It didn't feel like my money; I hadn't realised I'd won it: what was there to lose? I was at the roulette table for at least an hour, in my own world, before I headed back upstairs to our room.

When I got there, Emma asked, 'Did you go back to Ashbourne to get the tea?'

'What tea?'

'You went to get coffee and tea?'

'Oh fuck – back to you in a minute.'

I'd completely forgotten what I had gone down for in the first place, I'd been that lost in the gambling.

I'd say I blew a grand in In Vegas. It didn't matter. I was loose in this gamblers' paradise and I loved every minute of it. I sat at a blackjack table with Emma. Jack Daniels everywhere. Smoking cigarettes. I don't smoke really but when I'm locked, I'll have a few. Everyone in top form. I'm chatting to people from all over the world. The best tunes ever are blaring out around the casino. We were going to Fiji for a week or two after this before heading on to Australia. Life could not be better.

And the money I won? I couldn't wait to get rid of it. It had no value to me. Somehow it felt dishonourable or dirty, like drug money. I've always pictured a big imaginary devil over a bookies with a crooked finger, saying, *Right, pal, you've had your fun, you enjoyed that, you bought all the lads Jägerbombs, you bought Levi jeans, you bought a few shirts – come in to me now and start losing your hole.*

Vegas opened a secret door. I would never really have gone to a casino before then except the very odd time to Swords or somewhere like that. Now a whole new world was presented to me.

Chapter 7

Australia

LEABHARLANN CO. CHILL DARA

The Irish have a long history of heading off to foreign lands, whether by choice or necessity. I discovered over the time spent in Australia with Emma in 2010 that I was most definitely happier at home. We went there in 2008 to see Carol and Bren and I enjoyed it then, but I enjoyed it because I knew I was going home. By the end of the second trip, which lasted for the best part of a year, I couldn't wait to get back to Ashbourne. I knew I couldn't stand in Emma's way and any misgivings I had I needed to put to one side. It was the right time. Leaving my home club and my family was a wrench but I could not deny Emma something she'd set her heart on.

Not that it was all bad. After Las Vegas we visited LA before moving on to Fiji, which I loved. I learned a lot from being around the Fijians. They are the most positive people you could hope to meet. Every few months their houses get destroyed by a tsunami or hurricane or some other natural disaster and back they come each time to build them back up again. They're just very upbeat people and it rubs off on those around them.

We stayed on one of the islands for a week. And of course, exotic as Fiji is, we met two lads from Tipperary. One lad was a ringer for Pat Shortt. He was white as a ghost, naturally pale, one of those who in a place like Fiji, with its burning sun, spreads sun cream all over his body, and now I mean a thick layer of factor 50. He was lying on the beach one day and fell asleep and after he woke up, came up to join us at the bar.

'Jesus Christ lads! I got fucking burned', While he thought he had taken the usual care in covering his whole body from the sun he had forgotten, understandably, to apply sun cream on his eyelids. And for that small oversight during his nap he burned the eyelids off himself. 'Jesus lads! Every time I blink my eyelids are killing me.'

We took a boat out to the island where the movie *Castaway* was filmed, which sounds like heaven, of course, only there was no protection screen on the boat and I'd only a little bit of sun cream on me. I had no T-shirt either, I went bareback. Now spot the Paddy. One of the worst experiences is that feeling of getting burned and not being able to do anything about it. There was no way of escaping the blazing sun. I just had to take the heat.

And by god was there a price to pay for my stupidity. That night, I'll never forget, the pain was so severe I couldn't even drink to smother it. Emma was sunburnt too, though she did manage to drink plenty to numb the pain. But later that night, the drink wearing off, she woke up roaring her eyes out with the pain. My skin was bubbling up and the only temporary relief was to be found under a cold shower. The problem was that the second you stepped out of the cold shower the pain was excruciating. Of course, they warn you about it. But I didn't pay sufficient heed. Ah, sure, I'll be grand. That approach does not work in Fiji sun.

Even the next day, walking to breakfast, the minute the sun made contact with your skin the pain was agonising. You had to move in the shade. Step out under the sun and it was like being blasted with a blow torch. This ordeal took around three days to pass and then the skin started to peel away in great big swathes. But despite our soreness, we enjoyed Fiji and shared a memorable night with the locals where I ended up singing Luke Kelly's 'A Song for Ireland'. They loved it. Singing Luke Kelly songs is not unheard of when I've had a few pints.

With those preliminary excursions out of the way, we ventured on to Sydney. The plan was to stay with Carol and Bren for a couple of weeks until we got jobs and found our own place. Bren is a qualified engineer and he was loving life over there. Back then they lived in a small place called Neutral Bay.

Emma landed a decent job pretty quickly, so the three others in the house would head off to work and I'd be still at home looking for one myself. I quickly got homesick. I remember one day being out for a run and I had too much time to think and started getting physically ill, and was mystified as to the cause. After some time spent googling the subject I discovered that homesickness actually exists: missing home can make you ill. I was ringing my mam most days. I'd be constantly ringing the lads about how the football was going. I was out of my comfort zone. This wasn't me. In a deliberate way, in case I got to like Australia, I didn't let myself settle.

And I was still gambling. I found a place called Star City. I loved this place, a mini Vegas. Casino. Beer. Craic. Emma, Carol, Bren and I would be heading out at the weekend and I'd want to go to Star City. Too often. They'd be saying, 'Rory, we're on the far side of Sydney, why would we go to Star City?' They must have known I had a problem. Why else would I keep wanting to go there?

If you lost A$200 you'd say you'd lost only A$100. That's what you do. Bren had a small online betting account. He dealt in tiny amounts and only played sporadically. He would play blackjack at 50 cent a hand. One day he was there playing away on the laptop and I was half-watching telly and I said, 'Ah give us a shot at that there, Bren.' I think there was around A$40 in his account. He handed it to me and I'd say by the time he made the tea and came back the A$40 was gone. I said, 'Fuck this 50 cent bollocks.' I went up to a fiver, bump, lost the fiver, up to a tenner, bump, lost the tenner, and before I knew it, 'Oh Jaysus Bren, sorry I pressed the wrong button. Where's the money gone?'

Instead of admitting it, I had lied and said I must have hit the wrong button. And I used to laugh it off when I'd be in the casino, about how much I lost. I didn't have the ability to say, 'Right, I've had enough, I'm out of here.' I was too engrossed. I was hooked.

Emma was a huge fan of *Home and Away* and one day we decided to get a bus to Palm Beach, about an hour away, to see where they film it. When we got there Emma decided to do some sunbathing and I went for a walk along the water's edge. The big waves are unpredictable and I got hit by one – it was like a big jostle and I thought nothing more of it. We went for lunch and when I went to pay, I discovered my wallet was gone. I remembered the wave hitting me; I was wearing shorts and it must have been swept into the sea. I somehow blagged my way out of trouble in the restaurant, got their details and we did a bank transfer later to pay for the lunch.

But the wallet also had the bus tickets to get back home. So we're stuck there. Half an hour passed as we wondered what to do. Emma wasn't happy.

'You're an eejit! You have no responsibility.'

'That's not going to bring the wallet back. Let's think about this.'

I said we would get on the next bus, ticket or no ticket. She said we couldn't just go on without a ticket like that.

'Emma. I'm going back to Sydney. If you want to stay, do so. I'm getting on.' I was wearing the shorts, a Meath jersey and a pair of flip flops.

The bus came. I turned to Emma. 'Are you coming or staying? I'm going.'

'Oh my god you're so embarrassing!'

'Come on!'

So we got on the bus. Packed. I went up to the driver.

'How's it going, sir? My name is Rory, I'm from Ireland, I was down at Summer Bay beach, a wave hit me, lost my wallet, I've no money and I have to go home. Any chance of a free lift?'

And he looked at me and goes, 'Excuse me?'

'I swear to god, I got hit by a wave, we were there for the *Home and Away*, didn't see any actors, big fans, I have no money, I'm after getting a bollocking off the missus, please let us on the bus.'

And he goes, 'I don't often do this … but OK.'

I turned to Emma. 'Now Emma, sometimes in life you just have to be fucking honest. Let's go get a seat.'

And we got the bus home.

Carol eventually managed to land me an interview for a job similar to the one I'd had in Quinn Direct. We went off shopping and bought a 150-dollar suit. As well as the Quinn interview went for me, this was a whole different ball game. The sun was coming in through the window right on the top of my bald head and the sweat was already flowing when these two women came in and I knew by the heads on them that this was not going to go well. My charm wasn't working, I could see that straight away.

They started presenting these scenarios, asking questions, and I hadn't a clue what they were on about. I tried to small-talk my way out of it but unlike the girl back in Quinn Direct, when knowing her friend helped save me, there was no prospect of a repeat performance here. We were just staring at each other, no chemistry. I knew I was going nowhere. The more I talked the deeper I dug the hole. The nonsense that was coming out of me. Soon I lost all my confidence. I didn't know what to say. At this stage my whole back was drenched in sweat. I couldn't wait to get out of there.

Eventually I just said, 'We all know this isn't going particularly well and there's no chance of you hiring me, so if you don't mind I'm absolutely sweating here, can I please leave?'

They said OK. I shook their hands with the big sweaty paws on me, walked out onto the street, rang my sister and told her I was going on the building sites.

I registered with an agency – a gun for hire – and got a job as a labourer on a site in Balmoral, a Sydney suburb. If you're no good they won't ask you back. I approached it determined to make a positive impression because I needed to make some money. Simon was my boss, a Kiwi, nice fella. The construction site was on the grounds of a huge private residence owned by multimillionaires, overlooking Balmoral beach. I still have a class photo of myself leaning on the scaffold in the sun.

So Simon met me on the first day, and introduced himself.

'Rory, can you lay blocks?'

'Oh yeah, no problem.'

'I have a garden wall out here, the block layers have gone, there's only two rows, would you mind finishing it?'

'Yeah, no bother.'

So I went out and mixed a bit of mortar. I knew how to

do that much. Tony back in Ireland is an excellent block-layer and I'd often watched him at work. He has this knack with his wrists where he can flick it off the trowel. I can do that, like Tony, I reckoned. I started messing with the trowel but it went everywhere so I started gathering it with my hands. I laid about four blocks when Simon said, 'Rory, are you sure you've block-laid before?'

'I haven't, but I wouldn't say no to any work, boss.'

'Oh no, I appreciate that, fair play, but do you mind leaving that?'

So I left it.

He knew I was limited but still he managed to find something for me to do. No matter where you are, there's always someone who will try to find the good in you. He needed about 300 solid cavity blocks taken to the top floor. And the crane was away at this stage so I was delegated that task.

Now this was hard work. I started off carrying two at a time. I was going up four flights of stairs, maybe 80 steps, with these blocks – two cavity blocks, one in each hand. But I loved it, looked on it as physical exercise. I got a great buzz out of hard work and breaking a sweat. I don't know what it is about physical exertion, and perspiration, but I've always found it a great stress relief, as if a burden is being lifted from your shoulders. This simple labour perked me up. It helped me ease my homesickness. I just pushed myself to the limit and worked right through the day. It was enough to leave Simon impressed by my enthusiasm for hard work.

He asked me back the following week. I wasn't on great money but I was doing OK.

But the job that I feel stood to me then, and would stand to me for the rest of my life, came soon afterwards. At the rear of this house a concrete wall had been built with steel stabilisers running through it. You are looking at three or four feet of solid cement and internal steel cable. The home owner had decided she needed a balcony built at the window of one of her bedrooms. The wall was in the way, it had to go. They couldn't get the bulldozer in to get rid of this obstacle. So the boss told me that he had hired two Kango hammers and lined up another fella to come in to give me a hand.

'Now Rory, this is not going to be easy work, so take your time with it,' he added.

I'm not messing. I had to physically lift the Kango up on to my leg, hold it there and 'Kango' this wall. After a hard day's work, I was moving maybe only four inches of it, that's no word of a lie. I think I went through about ten Kangos, they just kept burning out. I went through around seven or eight assistant labourers who were working with me but couldn't stick it for very long before throwing in the towel. You had lads coming in who were just seeking a handy bit of work to keep the parents happy. Very quickly they were saying, 'The fuck am I doing this!' I wouldn't have done it at home. But I needed this job and I needed the money.

And I got to like the challenge, and the ferociousness of

the labour. I worked with gritted teeth for maybe six weeks to get the job done. That was all I did. From 7.30 a.m. to 3.30 p.m. each day. You'd drill like hell for a while and then stop to gather yourself, catch your breath and rest your limbs. It was physically the most brutal work I've ever done. My dad came over to visit and I brought him down to see it. I'd never had a test like it. My back was killing me. My shoulders were ready to collapse. The sun, 35 degrees, was beaming down on top of me. I lost two stone in weight, went from 17.5 to 15.5 in the space of weeks. I was eating little, mainly drinking water.

It soon occurred to me that, aside from it being a means of making money, I was taking my frustration out on this concrete wall, and the fact that I was thousands of miles from home and missing my family and friends. This was therapy, Kango style. Every day at 3.30 p.m. I left this punishing work, walked down to the beach and jumped in. And I can only describe the sensation as heavenly. I often sang 'Raglan Road' or 'The Town I Loved So Well' on the way, to make the connection with Ireland. Where I wanted to be. It was a kind of comfort. And I was only a few months into the trip.

You took a while to adjust to different things over there. At ten o'clock on one of the first mornings on the site someone said, 'Rory, we're having smokey.'

'Ah you're grand, I don't smoke.'

'No, fucking Irishman, it's breakfast.'

Now and then, drilling through this concrete wall, you'd

hit a steel rod and had to get out another heavy implement to cut through it. Then every day you had to load up the wheelbarrow and take the masonry to the dump and go back the next day and start all over again. I'd say the only way thing you could compare it to is doing hard labour in prison. But I actually enjoyed the intensity of the physical work, the total absorption in something, the lack of distraction.

During a breather you might think of something that annoyed you and then you'd go at it again. Drilling like a lunatic. It goes back to the days when I had a boxing bag in the shed when I was a teenager that I'd tear into most days. The same result achieved in releasing anger and frustration. I might think of that bollocks of a teacher I had back in school. Then I'd pick up the Kango hammer and let that concrete wall have it.

Talk about building up core strength – I was in some shape after a few weeks of this. I was ripped from the work. I'd come home, having done a hard day's work and soaked my limbs in the sea, take a shower and sit out in the evening sun and feel like a king.

I'd stop off on a Friday for a few beers and a few bets. Over there they have the bar and bookies in the one building. You go in and order a schooner of beer and bet away to your heart's content. Whatever was available. They had these horse and carriage events, the worst of all because if you're not in the front two at the start you have no hope. But it was enough to give me that fix. Then there was dog racing. In Australia there's eight dogs, two more than here, so it's hard enough for your dog to get to that first bend out in front. It's a lottery. If your dog makes it past the first bend without being nailed with a shoulder into the stand you have a chance.

So I was tipping away, again never mad money, but still feeding the habit. I might lose A$100, I could also win A$100, I couldn't afford to lose any more. I'd have five or six schooners and head home in the best of form and have a bit of dinner with Emma, who usually finished at 6 p.m., over two hours later than me. We'd have a few drinks together. That was my day.

I was as happy as I could have been in Australia at that point because I had a routine that kept me busy. I chose not to stay around Bondi Junction or to transfer to a team over there because of this fear I might get too cosy and want to stay. For the same reason I wouldn't allow myself to mingle too much with the Irish. So we stayed in a place called Crows Nest where we rented a house off an Indian man and shared with some people from India. We were the only Irish staying there.

On the odd Sunday we'd go to Bondi Junction where we'd hear the famous Bacon and Cabbage, this popular duet, two lads going flat out on the fiddle and the guitar. There was Irish food available and I loved all that. But I didn't want to settle or get too attached. I wanted a little piece of it, not enough to develop an addiction where I'd need it all the time.

To have something else to do, I looked up the local AFL

team in Crows Nest. I remember just rocking down for pre-season training one day. I considered myself fit, if never the most athletic, although I always had to work hard to get myself fit enough to play for the club at home. I never got the hang of kicking that Aussie ball in the short time I spent with this group of players, and trying to hop it was out of the question.

On one of my early days down there they had a time trial based on a 3k run. I identified around three lads that looked slightly out of shape and made a vow that I would at least finish ahead of them. My sister and Emma had come down to watch. So we took off. We did a lap of the big oval and then headed out a gate, up a street and back around a circuit they had mapped out. My strategy was to make a strong start, move to the front, figuring that most of them were going to pass me out at some stage. So for the first kilometre I ran and ran and one by one they started to overtake me. I was struggling to breathe and they were having open conversations as they ran by me. Then all of a sudden the three lads I had my eye on as the least fit all passed me out. I thought, *Don't let them out of your sight!* But soon I realised they were gone. So they all had come back in and were stretching and Carol goes, 'Where's Rory?'

Finally, I came around a corner, gasping. Emma recalls me protesting, 'They're freaks!' I had to get my inhaler.

I trained with them for a while but never played a match. If I got a ball, I just wellied it. Trying to pick a lad out? Forget about it. They were like a club team at home, close knit. Two or three of their best players would play the level just below AFL, VFL, and they stuck out a mile.

I was facing that concrete all day and then mixing with these players a few nights a week. It kept my mind off home. When they went on a weekend trip away, I cut my ties, I didn't want to get too close. I had it in the back of my head that I was going home for the championship in 2011.

During my time in Australia I had another one of those episodes caused by having weak bowels, like I'd previously had on holiday in Greece in 2005 when I had to dive into the sea and relieve myself while on a boat with no toilet. Manly is the area in Sydney where my cousin Dee and her husband Felipe live with their family and we were going out there to meet them around Christmas, along with my parents, who were over for a few weeks. Before we left I had a massive feed of spuds and a few pints of diluted orange. I had gone to the doctor before about my bowels. He said I just needed to manage them and avoid big dinners when not near a toilet. Basic enough advice. Anyway, I'll never forget it. Emma rang me, said the bus was leaving in ten minutes. I got into a lovely pair of shorts, a lovely shirt, and off we went.

We all got on the bus for the journey of about a half hour to Manly. The bus was packed and I was seated facing my dad and mam and Emma was alongside me. Ten minutes into the bus journey I felt that rumble. *Oh dear Lord, no.* And then the sweat was starting. And then I let out the most outrageous fart, a pre-warning. My Dad says, 'Did you fart?'

'Oh sorry, Dad, but that's the least of my worries at the

minute to be honest with you.'

Emma goes, 'Are you alright?'

'I'm not actually, here we go again.'

'Hold it.'

'I can't.'

And all of a sudden it started coming. So Emma and I jumped off the bus at the next stop and sprinted into a garage. I removed the shorts and boxers, washed myself down. Shorts back on. Got on the bus and went on to the cousin's place.

I went to another doctor in Sydney about it. I firmly believe the Ma overfed me as a young lad and the bowels couldn't cope. The two bowls of porridge every morning before school. It's the worst thing ever. It's like a 90-year-old man shitting himself in an old folk's home. Here I am, at 23, needing a nappy.

I don't care about telling people this. The reason I got into comedy was because I had no problem sharing disaster stories. Who cares? We're all going to be dead at some stage. Nobody gives a fuck really.

Meanwhile, the job offers also got shitty, literally. A sewage pipe burst in a restaurant and I was sent in to clear it. Had to pull up the floor. I can't begin to describe the smell. I rang my sister and told her what I was doing, and she said that I didn't need money that much, to please come home. I did feel fairly bottom of the barrel then, I admit. I did half a day and left.

About a week later on a really wet day I was told to be on

a certain site for work. It would be like living in Ashbourne and being told to go out to Sandymount on the southside of Dublin. So a bus into town and a Dart out, something similar. I left at maybe 5.30–6 a.m. and got there at 7 a.m. To find the site closed. Not a sinner around. So I rang the agency, asked if there had been a mistake,

'Oh sorry, Rory, forgot to ring you, they're off today, can you come back tomorrow?'

'Am I getting paid?'

'No you only get paid when you do the work.'

'Are you joking me?'

At this stage I hadn't that much money. And I was out in the back arse of nowhere, I didn't know where I was. It started raining. And when it rains in Australia, it really rains. None of these showers we get here. You'd be drowned in seconds. All of a sudden, the skies open up and there's me in my hard hat, and my boots and my little vest and the rain belting down. And I remember thinking, *Fuck this Australia craic.* I rang home in Ashbourne, told them I'm going back, had enough.

I got a bus directly to where Emma was working in Sydney, and sat on a bench outside her office building, soaked to the skin. We arranged to meet during her lunch break. I waited there, feeling sorry for myself, until she appeared.

'I'm going home.'

'What?'

'You can stay in Australia. You have a grand cushy job

there. I went to the back end of Sydney and got fucking wet and they're not even paying me. I'm going home. I love you and I'll see you in six months. Good luck.' And I started walking on.

She caught up with me and calmed me down. I think I did another eight weeks and then that was it. I was not for turning this time. I lasted ten months in total. We'd planned to be away for the year. We got our tax back and went home.

We arrived back in Ireland in August and I immediately focused my energy on trying to help the club win the senior football championship. They had qualified for the quarter finals.

I was only home four or five days when we had a match in the league against Walterstown. Now Andy McEntee had been on to me while I was away, he knew where my heart lay, so he started me midfield. Threw me right back in. As fit as I thought I was, when you haven't been training you fall behind. I struggled to keep up with the pace of the game and didn't play well. They took me off with ten minutes to go. A reality check. And I remember coming home from the game, I had these bands on my wrists, the likes the tourists bring home, and I cut them off in disgust. I had this beard and I shaved that off later too. That was a way of declaring that I needed to forget about where I had been and focus on what was ahead. That I meant business.

I got back training with the lads and we played Dunboyne

Me and Granny O'Connor. I was born on 17 March 1987, and unfortunately she passed away exactly three months later on 17 June. By all accounts, she was some woman.

My second birthday, surrounded by a few of the O'Connor clan.

Off to do some farming with my Grandad Daly and my sister
Carol. I officially started Rory's Stories on his anniversary –
4 November. He has definitely brought me some luck!

A bould head, holding my best pal,
Ted. Wherever I went, Ted came
with me.

Up on Grandad Daly's tractor. Although I grew up in a housing estate, farmers' blood runs through me.

My first day of primary school. I was terrified! As it turned out, me and school never did get on.

The successful Donaghmore-Ashbourne under-13 team of 1999. Not too hard to pick myself out! (*Courtesy of Tom Keenan*)

I played lots of golf as a young chap. Here is the first Ashbourne Golf Club under-15 team. I was 11 in this photo. (*Courtesy of Ashbourne Golf Club*)

Sharing a joke with my mam. She is always there for me.

With my godmother, Jeanie, on my
confirmation day. I could have passed
for a 20-year-old.

A family holiday in France in 2002. Great times.

Austin, Padraig Durkan (Durko), Tony and myself on one of many nights out.

Me and Emma in 2006. Young love!

On holiday in Greece in 2006. I was fit as a fiddle back then!

The 2003 Leinster Schools Final. The only thing I enjoyed in school was playing football. (*Courtesy of John Quirke Photography*)

With my dad on the morning of my debut for the Meath minors in 2004. He was very proud of me for playing for the county.

Bursting out with the ball during the Leinster minor quarter-final against Kildare in 2005. A very proud day captaining my county. (*Courtesy of John Quirke Photography*)

The winning 2007 Donaghmore-Ashbourne intermediate team. One of my favourite days playing football. (*Courtesy of John Quirke Photography*)

Our first senior championship match in 50 years. We defeated Kilmainhamwood that day. (*Courtesy of John Quirke Photography*)

Launching a ball into the Navan O'Mahonys square during the 2008 division 2 league final. (*Courtesy of John Quirke Photography*)

A born messer! Myself and Emma enjoying the Whitsunday Islands in Oz in 2010.

Me and Padraig (Sharkey) Finn during my tour of Oz in 2016.

Myself and Andy McEntee enjoying some lunch. Andy is a man whom I have the utmost respect for. He was there for me when I needed him most.

Paddy and me all togged out for yet another Rory's Stories sketch. We had some craic making them, especially in the early days.

Meeting the great Paul O'Connell in Lahinch in 2019. The first time I was ever star-struck! A true gentleman.

What a night! Celebrating Shane Lowry's win in January 2019. With AP McCoy, Alan Clancy, Shane, Robbie Keane and Lar Kinlan. All very sound men.

Performing to a full house in Vicar Street, September 2019. A 'pinch me' moment.

My two kids, Ella and Zach. I'm very proud of them.

Family means everything to me. Enjoying a holiday with the gang in Portugal in 2019.

in the quarter finals and hammered them. I only got on for the last ten minutes, which I accepted because I was only back a few weeks and the lads were going well. That set us up for a semi-final shot at Dunshaughlin in Pairc Tailteann in Navan.

I think it was one of the club's worst losses during my time playing. We were seven or eight points up at half time and lost by a point. We weren't going well at midfield. I was nearly begging Andy to put me on. John Crimmins, who I would have marked a lot, a big strong fella, was throwing his weight around for Dunshaughlin in the middle of the field. I felt I could quieten him. Andy brought me on for the last eight or nine minutes, which left me raging; I felt I should have been on sooner. We had to finish out the league so there was training the following Tuesday. I turned up but I refused to train. Instead I wanted to have it out with Andy. I told him I should have got on sooner. So we had an exchange. Proper argument. We're very good friends, but I felt I had dragged my girlfriend home early from Australia for this. Looking at it coldly, as Andy had to, I was only going to offer so much with the limited time I had been training and the lack of match practice.

When the football isn't going well, you feel it more if the other things in your life are not solid. Emma was unhappy that we had come home early from Australia, asking, quite justifiably, what for? When you're so engrossed in the GAA you have the blinkers on and in fairness to Emma she had sacrificed so much for me over the years because of football and the one thing she wanted to do was go away. And I'd dragged her home early. And we didn't win the championship and all I got was a measly ten minutes. The economic recession was still being felt here when we arrived back. That's when the depression really started to hit.

And of course Dublin won the All-Ireland that year, which didn't help.

Chapter 8

Under pressure

Once we'd been back in Ireland for a few weeks, Chris Bradley, my old colleague from Quinn Direct, directed me towards another call centre, this time for the ESB. The job was basically to ring people who weren't paying their bills. The location in Ballycoolin was only 20 minutes away, but the wages were diabolical, maybe €19–20k a year. It was a tough number. You were on a dialler system. It went beep and I'd look up and say, 'Can I speak to Joe Bloggs please?' Then I'd have to get them to confirm their name and address for data protection. Then I'd tell them they owe €50 on a bill and you can only imagine the height of abuse I got. Oh my god. I rang one particular fella.

'Hello, can I speak to John?'

'Speaking.'

'Hello, it's Rory here calling from ESB Networks, how are you?'

'What do you want?'

'OK, sir, can I have your name and address for data protection?'

'You know where I live – what's wrong with you?'

'I need your address for data protection.' So he gave me his address. 'Just to say your call is being recorded for data protection reasons. There is a technician coming out to your house today to disconnect you as you haven't paid your ESB bill.'

'What's your name, son?'

'My name is Rory.'

'Well, Rory, I'm sure you're a nice fella but would you mind passing on a message to the technician?'

'Yeah, no problem.'

'You tell the technician if he puts one foot on my land, I'm going to blow his head off with a shotgun. Is that fair enough?'

And I went: 'Do you mind if I put you on hold so I can speak to a manager?' I actually had to write down that we were being threatened with a shooting. That was rural Ireland for you. Some raw people I dealt with.

I remember ringing a fella in Dublin. He was an arsehole.

'I bet you're only on about eight euro an hour ringing me.'

'If you continue to abuse me I'll hang up the phone.'

'Yeah yeah, but not my fault you're on a shite wage.'

A horrible job does nothing for your self-esteem. I nearly got sacked a few times for muttering under my breath. The first time I experienced proper depression was in that job. I was prone to spells of poor form anyway – it was in my genetic make-up – but the horrible job was contributing to it, as well as a growing gambling problem, which I'd managed to keep largely hidden.

For a few years Emma would sometimes have come into the bookies with me. She didn't pass many remarks, seeing it as a hobby, nothing serious. But then around 2011 or 2012 there was a realisation that this was no longer something that could be ignored. One day in the kitchen I took a scissors to the gambling account card I had at the time. 'That's it, I'm done,' I said to Emma.

She got on to me about online betting, saying it was too easy, that I was sitting on the couch losing money we couldn't afford to lose. We were renting. She would have put the guilt trip on me, asking when were we ever going to have our own house. Emma worked in AIB at the time, she warned me about applying for a mortgage and that if you have any kind of betting record in your account over the past six months you're rejected right away. It was a constant source of friction between us. I stopped the online betting.

So I got this other card, which you could top up – if you won a few hundred you could transfer the money from that into your bank account, which I rarely did. Then I cut up that card, stayed off it for a few weeks. Then it would be the Masters. Or the All-Ireland final. Then, like anything, you get a win and you're back into it and lying again.

Maybe it was an escape from a job I hated. I remember distinctly the time I had to work after Christmas, pencilled-in for duty on 27 December. Undeterred, I drank the head off myself on St Stephen's Day. Michael Murphy, a family friend, worked there and picked me up at 8.30 that morning. He was fresh. I was violently hungover.

I got to work and logged in and I was just was ringing people and getting abuse and then I snapped. *I'm getting out of here.* I went up to the supervisor and said I was leaving. Despite being warned that I could get the sack, I walked out the door. I rang every person I knew and nobody answered so I started to walk home from Ballycoolin to Ashbourne. I walked maybe two miles before I got through to someone. And as god is my judge, I wanted a car to hit me. I was that dispirited. I know alcohol had a lot to do with it. None of my friends would answer and I needed to talk to someone to reassure me everything was all right. But I just wanted a car to hit me. Maybe not kill me, but put me out of my misery.

Colm Doherty finally answered one of my calls. 'Doc', as we called him, played hurling in the club for years, and I explained to him the scenario and he picked me up and brought me home. I often say to Doc that he doesn't understand how much I needed that lift home. Anything could have happened to me that morning, I was that low. I had just come home from Australia. I was in a dead-end job. And the drink was in me as well. That was a horribly low place. After a written warning, I went back to the job.

Our daughter Ella was born just after 2 p.m. on 29 October 2012, a bank holiday Monday, in Holles Street. It was a bit surreal in the labour ward. While Emma was pushing, I could hear a load of people outside on the streets cheering loudly because the Dublin City Marathon was on the same day and the runners passed by the hospital. Another coincidence was that later that same day Ballymun Kickhams won the Dublin senior championship for the first time in about 30 years, backboned by all those lads that I would have got to know: Philly McMahon, Davy Byrne, Elliot Reilly, the Dolan brothers, Alan Hubbard, who I first came across when I was a kid. If I'd transferred to Ballymun, who knows, I could have been part of that panel. Be just my luck to have the birth of a child and a county final falling on the same day.

I had another weird thing in my head. I was convinced that the year Ballymun won Dublin we were going to win Meath because we had some great battles with them in a tournament we'd play in Garristown where it was always nip and tuck. At that time I had a big row with Barry McCarthy, a brother of the Dublin player James, which led to a bit of a melee. Unfortunately, the year Ballymun won we were beaten in the semi-finals by Navan O'Mahonys by a point. It was sickening. I thought we'd win Meath and meet Ballymun in the Leinster Championship. Now, there's a good chance they would have wiped the floor with us. Anyway, it wasn't meant to be.

Ella's birth was very emotional and I remember shedding a tear. I would have been a young enough father at just 25. Since we'd come back from nearly a year in Australia in 2011, Emma and I were living separately in our respective family homes and I had a good bit on my plate. I was struggling with my mental health. Ella was a beautiful distraction from all the stress but it also made me realise that there were now added responsibilities. I had a child to look after.

Before the birth I didn't know what to expect. A friend said I'd cry and I told him I wouldn't be like that. And when you're in the labour ward, you feel like you can't do anything right. I think every man can relate to that feeling of total uselessness. You are sitting there encouraging your wife. And she is struggling. Then the magic when the child is born. I know I cried, I couldn't stop. Even Emma was laughing at me. I just could not stop crying.

And you have massive respect for women and what they go through. I used to think a kick in the bollocks was the worst pain you could go through. I'd probably accept that having a baby is worse.

Once it happens, you get that feeling that it is no longer just about you, I suppose every parent can relate to that. Knowing that you have to be responsible. Emma stayed in the hospital that night and of course I rang Tony and a few of the boys and we went on the beer up in the club until about four in the morning. Went back in to the hospital the next day to collect the Emma and the baby.

Having Ella meant I had to face reality. It became a matter of pride and necessity. Around then we couldn't even go down for a carvery on a Sunday in Ashbourne. We didn't have enough money after paying the rent. It's maybe €25–30 for a carvery lunch for two adults and we couldn't afford it. Going out on the beer was out of the equation. A few cans in the house would have to do. It was a miserable time. We'd no money and again I couldn't see myself ever having a good job. I was getting paid and putting bets on trying to win more money and that wasn't working.

In January I knew I had to get the finger out. My wage wasn't sufficient, so I worked hard to get a new job. If I had a profession it was probably as a credit controller. That's the area most of my work was in. So I rang loads of people. Got nowhere. But I kept trying. It was the first time I felt a sense of manly duty to find something better to provide for my family. To shake myself up.

We did the maths and I realised that €19–20k a year just wasn't going to be enough. During every break, I would be ringing loads of different companies, asking if they needed a credit controller. I remember sending my CV to a company in Ashbourne who I was full sure would give me the job and I never even got an interview. I don't know why. I rang loads of times, never got a phone call back.

For the first time in my life I felt real responsibility. I told myself: *You're a father now, your mam and dad have done a lot rearing you and worked hard and you need to do this for your family now. The ship has sailed for college, you may forget about that, and your fancy job and fancy car – no hope of that. Let's try our best and get a good job.*

A friend, Lauren Redmond, intervened. I would have hung around with her years ago. She's the daughter of Paul, our local barber. Obviously I don't give him too much business with my hair but he would be a good oul skin. Real old Dublin, good craic. So Lauren told me of this three-month contract in CPL, a recruitment company, for €28 grand a year, pro-rata. For me that was a huge jump in pay. Though it was advertised as being a three-month contract, I knew I could make it longer if I worked hard and made a good impression. *If I go in and work my hole off,* I thought, *they're not going to let me go.* And that's what ended up happening.

I had to do it for the family. I didn't want to feel like a useless father. I took nothing seriously except football but now I had to change. I wanted to be a better father for Ella. I didn't want to be that lying gambler, a selfish man. I wanted to raise her with proper morals, be someone she could look up to. And that's why now I'm very proud when Ella's friends ask her, 'Is your Dad Rory's Stories?' Stuff like that. And it makes me prouder still knowing that when she was in the womb it was a whole different ball game and I was living a different life.

I prepared properly for the CPL interview. I wanted this job. I did a strong interview, threw everything I had at them and got selected. It was a substantial difference in the wage and it meant we could have a carvery now at the weekend. I felt a little bit of a weight off my shoulders. I knew going in I mightn't have much of a clue what I was doing but I was willing to give it 100 per cent.

Because CPL was a big company, there was potential for career advancement. At this stage I'd probably resigned myself to the fact that this was where my future lay. *Rory, you're going to be a credit controller, but maybe try to be the best credit controller – maybe you can be a team leader one day?* Get to that €40 grand mark, which is a very liveable salary.

The workplace was on Merrion Square in central Dublin, in a small room containing me and my team leader John Heffernan and a guy called Adrian Carney, a rabid Leeds United fan and someone I got to know well. I'd learned valuable lessons from the GAA and particularly Andy McEntee, our manager when we won the intermediate championship, about the rewards of working hard. I was given a spreadsheet with loads of names and numbers on it. My job to begin with was to ring these people – starting at the top of the list – and tell them they owed CPL money. And put my notes into the comments section and move on. That was it.

I can safely say I gave it the most I have ever given any job. I worked really hard. The weekly call stats came up and I was doing treble what everyone else was doing. I was pretty sure there were lads there saying, 'Fuck, slow down, new boy, don't be showing us up here.' I had to make sure they gave me a contract: for me, this was do-or-die. I didn't miss a day. I worked ferociously for the first three months, did everything they asked. I licked arse. I was an absolute winner of an employee.

Then I got the full-time job. And that was great. And like most people I went into a comfort zone then and went backwards. I knew they couldn't sack me as easily now. But

I didn't have a passion for the job, I did it for my family and because I had to pay my rent.

And this is the job I had in 2013, when I hit rock bottom.

Chapter 9

Mug's game

When you start losing, the gambling addiction kicks in even more. In your head there's always a chance that you'll recover the money. Gamblers often say that putting the bet on is the most hypnotic part, not collecting your winnings. That little buzz of excitement waiting for the dogs to be released from the traps or for the horses to be released from the stalls. That energy rush when, say, you have Ruby Walsh in a race and you know he's cruising and you see him clearing the last and pushing on to the line. In those moments I never thought of the money, it was just the sheer thrill of the moment. *Ya fucking boy ya!* And what would often happen was, say I had €20 on Ruby, even money, and won €40, in the time I'd be up to collect my winnings I'd already be watching the next thing that moved. And it could be a virtual race. *Right, quick, a tenner on number five!* And I wouldn't have any hard cash, so I'd be handing the girl at the counter my docket to get the €40 to pay for the next race, and she'd be rushing because the race would soon be off. And then I'd get thick because she wasn't moving fast enough, the race had started – it was too late. And that's pure addiction.

Then the phone would ring. Emma.

'Are you in the bookies?'

'No, no. Just down here getting a roll.'

There are four bookies in our town. We had this thing of moving from shop to shop. You'd be in one of them and maybe not doing well and decide to go to a different one thinking you'd have better luck. And walk in as if you were starting with a clean slate, even though you were already down in reality. These delusional mind games were part of the game. After another hour of losses, you'd move to a new establishment and enter its doors as if you were a fresh punter with no history of failure. This self-deception went on for a long time.

And we'd be there on a Sunday for two or three hours and Emma would ring me from home. And I'd come out of the bookies and go down the lane to take the call. 'Oh, I was just over here for a walk.' You'd see grown men leaving the bookies when a call came in because they didn't want it to be known where they were.

Meath is a horsey county, which meant I had a few contacts. I knew Andrew Lynch, a successful jockey, and played football with his brother Martin. But I knew nothing about horses, even though Tony and I used to let on we had some knowledge. I hadn't a fucking clue what these oul lads who knew racing were talking about. I'd let on I was one of these horsey lads, 'Oh yeah, I hear the ground is firm in

Clonmel, and Ruby likes firm ground …' The fucking head on me. I just wanted a fix and that was it. Didn't matter what the sport was.

I was transferring wages into my bookies' account whenever I got paid. And that was a disaster. I would lodge €50 thinking that would do. If I was alone on a Saturday watching the racing, and noticed two more races coming up after all the money had gone, I'd rush to the bookies to put another €50 on. You might go in and someone would mention another horse and you'd switch bets. That loses, the money's gone. You go home raging with yourself.

It's a horrible feeling when you lose a good bit of money. You meet people on the way home and you have a normal conversation but really you just want to headbutt the wall. And those times walking from the bookies to my house, which was less than a five-minute journey, whacking myself full force in the face thinking, W*hat are you at, you absolute fucking eejit?* But then when I got to the door, I'd have to let on everything was grand.

I didn't lose astronomical amounts of money and I never borrowed to bet. But I was spending way too much in proportion to what I was earning. When I was being paid €1600 a month, and €800 or €900 was set aside for bills, shopping and all that, I might have €300 euro a month to play with. I was wasting money I couldn't afford to be throwing away.

After I'd earned a name with Rory's Stories and stopped gambling, a leading bookmaker offered me serious money to promote their brand, a job I felt I couldn't afford to turn down. I did two videos and a promotional gig for them and then called a halt. I couldn't go on. I told my agent I felt that after all I'd gone through it wasn't right and offered to pay back the money I'd already earned. I couldn't have it on my conscience and I deeply regret ever agreeing to do it in the first place. I've had lots of offers from the gambling industry since and I've turned them all down.

Online betting removes the stigma and dread of sneaking down to the bookies and the losses seem less damaging when there isn't a physical transaction involved. Now it was terrifyingly easy to lose money and become a slave to this private world. You never handled any money. It went electronically from your bank account to your bookies' account where it bided its time before it became the property of the bookmaker. The bookies even came up with a plastic card for its customers to make spending easier – the one I cut up with the scissors to make a point to Emma that I was breaking the habit. All of these were tricks to keep you under their spell.

Looking back, it seems terrifying how I behaved then and how much betting had me on a string. At night after Emma went to bed, I'd go looking for some sports activity. You might find a cricket match in God knows where and while I don't know a cricket ball from a cricket bat, I'd be betting on these lads to get so many overs on even money. And there

I'd be, glued to the cricket. I enjoy playing and watching golf but that was also fair game – I'd be betting fivers on Rory McIlroy or Shane Lowry to par the next hole and all this kind of stuff. If you said to me around then, 'Rory, there's two cats out there trying to get up a tree. I'll give you 2–1 on the black one', I'd be out there, totally engrossed.

To make matters worse, the Wi-Fi was never great in our house. There were Saturdays with no one home but myself and a race about to come on and I'd be up in the far bedroom, on top of the bed, with the phone at full stretch trying to get coverage to get this bet on. And I'd hear on the telly downstairs, '*We're off now in this two-mile novice chase …*' I'd swear like a sailor knowing the chance was gone. And heading back downstairs I'd know in my bones that this horse was going to win and of course it would win because I couldn't get the fucking Wi-Fi on. Torture.

Of course, there were good days. It wasn't all bad. Enough good days to keep me dreaming. I'd try a lucky 15 and if it comes with good odds, for just €15 I could win five or six hundred. Now once a year, if not every two years, this might happen. I'd go down to the bookies in top form, I swear to god, you can nearly hear the song, '*Why do birds suddenly appear …*' It could be raining and you'd be the happiest man alive. I'd go into the bookies and be, 'Howya, John! Alright, Tommy!' And I'd look up at the screen and there'd be racing on in Dundalk that night and I'd pick two horses and put a tenner on each and there could be soccer on and I'd put €50 on a game and go home and watch the horses romp home and my team win 3–0. So I would have made €700 that day.

Then I'd get up the next morning in mighty form, skip down to the shop, get a coffee, get a paper, start to pick out horses and probably wouldn't get a winner for another three weeks. And the €700 would be gradually reduced. And I'd go down another €200 before I won it back.

I often say in my talks that I'd love to go to Cheltenham and back horses and drink pints and leave it at that, but I can't, and I've accepted it. There's one person like me in every group. I used to love to have the house to myself, sit on the couch with a couple of bottles of beer and have €100 in my account and the *Racing Post* next to me and *At The Races* on the telly. I would be in heaven. I'd be like a heroin addict getting his shot. Or an alcoholic hitting the whiskey bottle. Even if I lost it all I'd get two hours out of that €100. That was enough.

I remember sometimes going to Blanchardstown with Emma and looking at a jacket or a pair of shoes for €100 and saying, 'Are you joking me? Put it back.' And then spending €100 in the bookies that evening. You don't really have any respect for money. I'd love to spend a Saturday sitting there doing that again, but I can't. I know it's not good for me, so I leave it. But when you're into gambling there's nothing better. No point in lying about it. I just can't do it anymore.

Tony recalls times at our house with his wife Jen and I'd only be half-listening to them. I'd be watching the racing. He knew then I'd definitely gone past the level we were at when we went betting together over the years. He often said, 'Rory, I'm telling you now, man, you need to stop that.' Tony was very supportive and a good, concerned friend.

I'd give it up for a month, think I was cured, then go back. I'd lose the couple of hundred euro and I'd tell Emma I'm not gambling anymore. I'd delete my bookies' app. I'd cut up the cards. And that'd be it. Then after some time had passed, I'd be lulled into a false sense of security. *I'm grand now, I'm just going to have a bet on the golf.*

I had a good moment when Bubba Watson won the Masters in 2012. I'd a fiver each way on him at 50–1 and he hit a key shot from the woods that went round onto the green. Happy days. And the following day when I went down to collect my winnings, I put €25 on Líon Na Bearnaí to win the Irish Grand National. Which he did. And so I won another €400. That's how it goes like. No bus for ages, then two come at the same time.

I even went through a phase of telly bingo. And at times I'd go into the bookies and just for a slight bit of a hit I'd pick three numbers in the national lottery and sit at home with my mother and pray to fuck the number eight comes out of the pot. Again, another fix. I needed a bet on to keep me going.

As I say, the event didn't matter in the slightest. I watched Longford Town against Sligo Rovers one day and sat through 90 minutes of pain, a nil–all, because I might have had €20 on Sligo Rovers. Swear to god, I didn't know any player and I was cursing every move they made. This lad might miss a

penalty and I'd fuck the remote control against the wall. I'd
no interest in this shit at all.

And then the GAA broke my heart because I thought I
knew what I was betting on there. It made no difference.
A little knowledge is a dangerous thing. Kilkenny might
be playing Wexford in the summer, and Kilkenny are just
Kilkenny, a safe bet. Along with that I'd have two horses, at
say even money, which is a gamble, and I'd throw Kilkenny
in at 1–4, for example. Because the thinking goes that if the
horses win it's €100 and Kilkenny will definitely win. So
the two horses romp home and somehow Kilkenny have an
off day and are bet by a point or they draw. And everyone
you meet is saying, 'Jesus, that was some performance from
Wexford!' and I'm saying, 'I know, the dirty bastards!'

My mates, we'd often slag each other over the near-
misses, the hard-luck stories. Like a scene unfolding on
Soccer Saturday when you're waiting for the last result in
an accumulator. All the teams winning near full time. 'And
there's a *goooaaal*, there's a *goooaaal!*'

'Please, *nooo* …'

They go to the team I'm waiting on. 'It was the flukiest
goal ever! One all!'

And I used to send a photo to the lads. *Guess who I was
waiting on?* And they'd be all laughing their heads off.

It fucks with your head because you go into all this
superstitious stuff. I'd be known as a jinx to the lads. Like
when we'd be in the bookies and I'd ask them who they
had and they'd never tell me because once they told me

the horse would fall. I was a jinx. Or we'd be watching a particular horse and I'd say, 'Jaysus, Tony, he's flying.' Next thing he'd fall and Tony would look at me ready to box me in the nose. When you're into gambling you're superstitious, you become a weirdo really.

I could have lost €200 and I'd go home to my mam and I'd ask her for a fiver to go to the shop to get something and I'd go down to the bookies with the fiver after losing €200. And that's when you know you've an issue. But I wanted to stop.

On a Thursday evening in early June 2013 we ventured to Simonstown to play Rathkenny in the championship, who are always tough to beat, a really dogged team. They had county players Brian Meade and Donal Keoghan to call on. Donal Curtis, who won All-Irelands with Meath in 1996 and '99, was there too and is still defying age, togging out for his club well into his 40s. We were beaten and I didn't play well, taken off in the second half. As a result my head was all over the shop. Losing in the championship leaves your spirits on the floor. Afterwards I'd head out with the lads and try to bury the pain in alcohol and consoling thoughts of the next match or year. But a loss like that, and a poor performance to boot, stays in the system. It's not quickly flushed away.

On the day following our defeat by Rathkenny, I met up with some people I used to work with. We headed into Dublin and went on the beer. Eoin Reilly, who I played a lot with at midfield for the club, joined us. We hit O'Donoghue's just off Suffolk Street. Conveniently, there's a bookies right beside it. Reilly fancied a bet but he wouldn't have been as engrossed as I was. He enjoyed a flutter, could take it or leave it.

That day I was running mindlessly in and out of the bookies. I was at a low point: I knew full well the grip my addiction had on me, the harm it was doing to me and my family, financially and psychologically. I was no longer free. I had responsibilities. I had a baby daughter and Emma was trying to run the home as best she could, but I didn't care about that or anything else. I craved the high that comes with the risk, that would make me forget about football, forget about life, forget about everything. All I wanted was to go on the piss and gamble. Over those hours in town, while on the face of it we were all having a great time, I was losing money heavily and couldn't stop myself losing more.

Later we went to a night club, I think somewhere on Camden Street. A friend of mine, Donal McDermott, was home from England and joined us. Donal played professional soccer over there. He's a good fella. When he comes home he's probably a bit too generous with his credit card. He put money behind the bar. There was vodka everywhere. Everyone was having the craic. But I didn't want to be there. My mind was elsewhere. I craved another punt, needed to find a late-night casino to try to get my money back. Could I sneak out, recover the losses and be back drinking with the lads before anyone realised I'd been away?

I knew, deep down, that this was madness. This uncontrollable desire to keep playing with fire, no matter how many burns I'd got from my previous escapades. My inner voice was telling me the folly of gambling beyond my means. I was having this conversation with myself over and over: *Rory, snap out of it. You know you're going to lose your bollocks if you go back down there. Just forget about the gambling and enjoy yourself with the lads.* But it was futile. The demon had me and was calling the shots. I'd made up my mind.

I turned to the rest of the crew. 'Listen, lads, I'm heading home.'

'Ah no, Rory, stay. It's still early.'

'Ah no, I'm wrecked, I've been on the beer all day.'

I said my goodbyes and left the club. And the gas thing about gambling is that the minute I started walking down the street towards the casino I actually got excited, I forgot about everything that had happened, being knocked out of the championship, the money I'd lost. It was a fresh start and I was going to win my money back. I think I had only €200 or €250 left in my bank account, I had paid the rent and given Emma money for shopping. But it was money I could ill afford to lose. I stopped at a cashpoint and took it out regardless. At the casino I went heavy straight away, put on maybe €100 or €125. I wanted my money back. I laid it on black in roulette and I hit red. Then I went for it again, and chose a different colour. I went for red and hit black. Just like that the money was gone and there were no other options. The bank account was empty. I think I might have had two or three euro in my pocket and that was me done.

Bewildered, I wandered through the casino. There were loads of people around the roulette and blackjack tables, in high spirits. All I could hear was people having fun. And as I walked through the room, it felt like I was having an out-of-body experience. Everything I had done had just hit me. *Oh my god, what are you after doing?* I remember walking outside the casino, it was lashing rain. A horrible night. With the rain coming down on top of me, I looked up at the sky and said to myself, *What's the point?* Those demons were relentless now. Y*ou're an absolute disgrace, Rory. You don't even have the football any more, you're shite at football. You're starting another crap job. You have a young daughter at home who is depending on you and a girlfriend who deserves better.*

All these negative thoughts came flying at me. And then I thought of suicide. It floated around there in my addled head for a while, making a home for itself along with the shame and the anger and the despair.

But two thoughts came to me now, like warning signals, and they were the lifelines I held on to.

My cousin took his life when he was 23 and now I thought of him and the devastating ripple effect it had on his immediate and wider family. The other jolting memory was more recent. The previous December, shortly before Christmas, Shane McEntee, a Meath TD, took his own life. His brother Andy, who managed us when we won the intermediate championship, was someone I held in the highest regard. Shane was buried in Nobber on Christmas

Eve on a lovely bright sunny day, with a huge crowd present. I went there to sympathise with Andy most of all. I remember standing outside the church and hearing Gerry McEntee, probably the most famous of the family, talk about online trolls and the impact they had on his brother's mental health. And he also said to ask for help if you ever feel like his brother did, not to have your family go through what they were going through. And that stuck in my mind.

Those two deaths left a deep impression on me and helped keep me safe. I took out my phone and rang my girlfriend.

'Emma … get me home now.'

PART 2

Chapter 10

Meltdown

I had no money to pay for a taxi. Nine times out of ten a taxi driver will ask you for payment up front if you're going back to Ashbourne from town. There's a good reason for that. People, myself included in the past, would have got the taxi back home, then left the driver in a cul-de-sac and jumped over a back wall. We were hoors for doing it. Not proud of it but that's what we did. This time I had a stroke of good fortune, maybe my luck was starting to turn, because when I said 'Ashbourne' he didn't ask for payment, he just replied, 'No bother – jump in.'

The journey home is all a blur. I don't know whether I spilled my heart to him, I was in such a messed-up state. We got home. Emma paid him the €50 and I went to bed and fell into a deep sleep.

On waking the next day Emma asked what the problem was. 'Ah, I said, just not myself. But I'll be alright, I'm grand.' Typical Irishman's answer.

She rang my dad and he arrived a few minutes later. I came downstairs like a little scared boy. And I sat there and he asked what was wrong and I just said, 'Dad, I'm not in a good place. My confidence is gone. I'm not enjoying football like I used to be. I'm gambling too much.'

'Really?' he said, surprised. Like, parents, even though they think they know their kids, they don't really know them. They would have known I enjoyed a bit of craic but they never would have known I was addicted to gambling, that things had gone so far down that road.

We talked about what to do, possible solutions. Andy McEntee came into my mind again. I could trust him. He had been through the mill with the loss of his brother. I picked up the phone and called him.

'Rory, how are you?' Andy is a very positive man. And I'd be a positive person too so he knew right away, by the tone of my voice, that there was something seriously wrong.

'I need to talk to you.'

'No problem, Rory, where are you now?'

'I'm in Ashbourne.'

'I'll meet you in Ratoath in two hours.'

Which, when you think about it, was amazing really. He dropped whatever he was doing. I drove over myself, still hungover as well, so I was depressed beyond belief. We met in a place called Ryan's. When I pass it now I still get the shivers from the memory it triggers of that day.

When I arrived he was already there to greet me.

'Rory, what's the story with you?'

He hadn't been manager of our club for a few years. He had moved on, he may have been with the Meath minors at that stage. We spoke for a bit about my confidence. About Donaghmore-Ashbourne, who I loved to bits, who were not going well. The dream of us winning a championship was gone, all this sort of stuff.

Then I mentioned gambling and straight away he said, 'Rory – that's the real issue.'

Andy had encountered a variety of people with gambling problems. And he told me a story about one man who got help and who's not allowed to buy even as much as a scratch card anymore. Then he said, 'Rory, I'm not an expert but I want you to meet Gerry Cooney.'

Now I would have known Gerry Cooney, he would have helped Andy out with Donaghmore-Ashbourne. A serious and respectful man, he knows his football. He also knows plenty about people. He worked in the Rutland Centre (the addiction treatment centre in Knocklyon), which I never knew until I had this conversation with Andy. Anyway, the next day I made the call to Gerry and we arranged to meet a couple of weeks later in the Red Cow Hotel on the outskirts of Dublin. He asked me to bring Emma along, which I was happy to do. I wanted everything out there on the table.

It was good to see him again. Once we'd all sat down, he asked me about myself and how the football was going, and said Andy had told him I was struggling with the gambling.

He spoke about various people; Niall McNamee was one name he brought up. I told him that I had read Niall's blogs recently and they had been very relatable, and that I'd enjoyed Oisín McConville's book *The Gambler* – I don't read too many books – and that it had made a big impression on me. Now I wasn't as bad as Oisín, not in as deep, but I could see I had the same mindset at times.

'Listen, Gerry,' I said. 'I want to be able to go in and have a few pints with the lads and not have one eye on the telly. And not have to wake up on Saturday morning and think about my accumulator that day and nearly skipping down to the shop to get my hands on the racing paper to check out the form.' I added that I knew fuck all about the horses anyway, I just pretended I did.

Then Gerry spoke for a while. He introduced me to the concept of negative and positive platforms – which I now cover at length in my talks. He noted that I have an addictive personality, which is absolutely true. I've had that from childhood.

He explained to me that the negative platform is where you find people who are struggling with various addictions such as alcohol, drugs, gambling – anything that can bring you up quickly and land you on your hole just as quick. People have been struggling with those issues since the beginning of time. They'll always be with us. We just need to know how to manage them, he added.

On the other side you have the positive platform, where some of the most successful people in the world are to be found; people who are immersed and thriving in their lives and in what they do. And he told me that I needed to get on to that platform. I needed to find something I was interested in to fill the void once gambling was removed from the equation. And it had to happen immediately. There was no point in saying you'll stop. You needed something to replace it.

So he suggested a few things. He knew I was into GAA and exercise. While he was talking, I thought to myself that I've always had a feel for acting and comedy. I was good at telling stories and making people laugh by just being myself. I wasn't afraid to tell a yarn. I rarely got embarrassed. I told a story and that was it.

The void was obviously to be filled with Rory's Stories. Although I wasn't to know that at the time.

He advised me to take it gradually. He gave me a month or two to eliminate gambling completely. And then you take each day as it comes and if you feel you are able to survive you keep doing it – but the key to that is finding something to fill the void, something else to think about. And he was right.

He gave me examples of former heroin addicts who take up exercise and now run several marathons a year. I often talk about a former chronic alcoholic who gave up drink and took up golf, and plays that two or three times a week to keep his head right. Sport is a valuable resource for people in weaning themselves off addictions. And having a routine is part of that. I consider myself a smart fella, I wouldn't be 'booksmart', but when it comes to understanding life and that, I consider myself pretty tuned in. I knew what Gerry meant straight away.

The meeting with Gerry lasted about an hour. There was no issue with concentration here, like in school, I was completely absorbed in what he was saying. I wanted to stop gambling so badly I listened to every word he said. I was a man on his knees asking for help. *I am down here. Whatever you tell me to do I will do.* One thing he suggested was going off the drink for a few weeks, which I did. I went on the dry for maybe two months. He was right. I actually got most of my urges to gamble when I was hungover, because that was a time I'd be feeling low and needed a pick-me-up. A lot of people can relate to that. When I woke up I'd get a breakfast roll and head down to the bookies with €100 and act the bollocks for the day. And that's woeful for your mental health.

And I began to understand and respect alcohol. I still drink, but only when I've nothing on. People might say, *why don't you give it up?* Because I don't think I need to, it's not that bad. I can manage it.

Meeting up with some of my best friends and going on the beer for the day with good Guinness and great craic and laughter – that's something I still enjoy and want to continue enjoying. But drinking ten pints just because you're not in good form on a Sunday evening? That's not worth it.

I have respect for teetotallers but there are some positive elements to drinking. It helps some people loosen up and offers a social outlet. I only got a message recently on social media from a fella who said he had watched one of my videos about opening up and not being in a good place. He was in a pub with his mate and the mate asked if he was OK. He said that he wasn't, and suggested they go and grab a bag of chips. And they spent an hour over taco fries talking about his feelings. He went home the next day and he told his parents what he was thinking. He wasn't exactly suicidal but just not himself, not happy. And his brother and sister came out and said the same thing. They felt like it but nobody ever spoke like that until he brought it to the table. That was revealed over a couple of drinks. But it can be a thin line with alcohol, I fully understand that.

The details of that time outside the casino, when I'd hit rock bottom, are fuzzy because of drink. I can't remember what was said when I phoned Emma beyond the fact that I felt terrible and needed to get home. She knows me – I wear my heart on my sleeve. I do remember that she told me to get home immediately. Not to do anything stupid. Get in a taxi. Get home.

There were a few tears. And I'd say it was a scary phone call for her. Like, this is three o'clock in the morning with a young child in the house. And she knows I'm a headbanger, wired up. And I wouldn't be ringing her crying every day of the week. I'm sure she was worried. I'd say when that taxi arrived and I got out her heart rate came down something shocking. I'm pretty sure she rang me halfway home in the taxi, just to make sure, which was great thinking from her because I was vulnerable at that moment in time. I don't think I would have taken my life to be honest with you. Because of my cousin and because of Shane. Because you often heard people speak about such and such taking their own life and they were the life and soul of the party. And I was that person. It put me on guard.

And I basically said to myself, *I'm not going to be another one of these stats.* Like, I have a cousin who suffers from depression. And he's been in and out of counselling. And he pretty much said because one of our cousins did it, that probably saved him from doing it.

I've seen an interview with a guy who was about to jump off the Golden Gate bridge. He was saying how, as he was preparing to jump, he was crying for help, hoping someone would intervene, that he didn't actually want to die, he just wanted someone to stop him. And that just as he jumped, the second he stepped off, he felt regret but it was too late. He broke every bone in his body but survived and was pulled alive out of the water. He said he remembers the doctor saying to him, 'Fifty-five people jumped into that river in the last month and you are the only person pulled out alive.'

And then he goes on to explain how he still gets it, the depression, and that he's been in mental-health facilities three times since. But he has reached an accommodation with that. And I too am starting to accept that I suffer from depression. It's not going anywhere. You understand it as best you can and manage it and know that it will pass.

When I feel the onset of that darkness, I go back to the drawing board. I delete social media for a day. I avoid any negativity I might see online, whether that's general comments or someone having a personal dig at me. Remove that toxicity straight away. Simple things and small steps. Eat well. Talk to someone I haven't spoken to for a while. And train like a dog. But you can't do it all on your own.

That's why I needed Andy when my depression was at its worst and for his help I will be forever grateful. He identified the gambling as the disease, the source of my ills, and told me that it was killing me, but that everything would improve if I tackled it. At the time the country was still in a recession, we were renting a house, trying to make ends meet. We'd a young child. We were a young couple. The pressure of life was ever present. I'd reached a stage where I was burnt out. I'd hit the wall.

For all the fear and shame I felt, I knew in my heart and soul I'd made the big step in admitting I needed help. I knew that from this moment onwards it was only going to get better. And I trusted Andy with my life not to tell anyone. Yet if you were to tell me then I would be where I am now, I wouldn't have believed it.

After that experience in Dublin I knocked all bets on the head. I was too afraid not to. I wanted to stop more than I wanted to breathe. I had ceased betting for stretches before, cancelled my accounts. I'd stop for six weeks but slowly return. I'd go back and put a fiver on a week, in an accumulator. What happens? That wins. Then you think you're grand again. You might say you'll just bet weekends. Then you are back at square one.

It is all or nothing for the addicted. Oisín McConville's book I'd read in three or four sittings. I was enthralled. Gripped. Everything he said was telling me, *oh Rory you have a problem, pal. He* was the heavier gambler: where he lost €5,000, I might lose €100. But it was still the same. He'd to go to bookies where nobody knew him. Once he lost a few grand and came back out to his car and hit the steering wheel in a fit of rage and frustration he was so pissed off with himself. And then he checked the car for loose change and found a few quid and went in and bet again. And I could relate to that.

I've often walked home after losing €200–300, boxing the head off myself until I got to the doorstep. But then I'd raid my dad's golf bag for spare change and go back down to the bookies and chance the six or eight euro. They got to know me in the bookies. They're no fools. They notice what's going on. They know you were in there two hours earlier putting tenners on, and that now you're back with 50 cent each way.

I get uneasy every time I drive past a bookies. I always think that there's one person in there who's exactly like I was, feeling worthless. And you do. You feel pathetic when you've lost your money and you walk out. And here was me with a shit job, a young child at home, renting a house; I can barely afford a carvery and here I am putting a bet on. What a joke. And that's where the demons really went at me until I stopped. And now you have teenagers using betting apps on their phones at school or in college who go on to lay bigger and bigger bets once they're earning a salary.

People need to realise the connection between gambling and suicide. A study in 2019 found that suicide rates increased 19-fold among men between the ages of 20 and 49 if they have a gambling problem. Peter McNulty used to play for Portlaoise and took his own life because of gambling. He got himself in debt, got himself out of it, fell back in and took his life. I met Peter a few times and I played against him once; a very good footballer, and a lovely fella. And between his death, between Niall McNamee's blogs and Oisín McConville's book, the implications of where I was and where I was heading began to sink in. So make no mistake: people talking about their own issues will help others. Because Niall helped me. Oisín helped me. And, unfortunately, Peter's death made me realise where I also could go.

When we got to the county final in 2014, I went into the bookies with the lads and I might have given a lad a tenner to put on a tip. That was as close as I'd been to betting since May 2013. This was the Monday after the game. We were drinking all day. That was stupid of me but I nipped it in the bud. I haven't placed a bet since.

I gave up the drink for a while. I didn't gamble. I did all they told me to do. From that May to November I watched very little sport on television or in person to ward off the temptation to gamble. Sometimes Emma and I would go out for a walk or a drive when a GAA match was on just to break that connection. You distance yourself from anything like that, as Gerry advised. You create a gap. But there was still the void and I needed an outlet for my energy. I had been toying with the idea of writing about comic episodes in my life, but I wasn't sure about the right medium. I talked to Emma in vague terms about doing comedy sketches and didn't follow through, but it would not go away. I just felt, deep down, that this was the area I wanted to explore.

In November 2013 the real magic began to happen. That eureka moment had arrived. I started to write a blog, funny stories off the top of my head, like I'd be telling countless times in company over the years. And people liked what they read. I began to build up a following. And now I was addicted again. I had the same tunnel vision that applied when I was gambling but this time it was doing me no harm. I knew in my bones that I had finally found what I was looking for.

Chapter 11

Rory's Stories

My cousin Bref Murphy, to whom I'm very close, half claims to have come up with the name 'Rory's Stories' – in any event, that was the name agreed on when I started writing a regular blog on Facebook in November 2013. For some months before, outside of the day job, which paid the bills, I'd been writing on random topics on my Facebook page and gauging public reaction. Like a series of dress rehearsals before the opening night. I could see that the response was positive. The early evidence suggested that there was an audience out there for the kind of humour I was peddling, these stories of everyday life that people could easily relate to. Bref was really positive too, a great motivator, as I tried to find my way. 'Go for it,' he'd say. 'You're a funny fucker – just go out and start telling stories.'

But it took time and patience to find the right platform. Telling stories was no bother to me. I'd told them countless times in pubs and around the GAA club right back to childhood and got plenty of laughs but this was a new venture. One of the first stories I chanced putting up on my

Facebook page was from a holiday in Greece with Emma in 2006. It was about a boat trip that went badly wrong when, while I was hungover to bits, the propeller on the boat failed and Emma and I were left baking in the hot sun out from the shore. All of a sudden there was an even greater emergency. I needed to go to the toilet and my bowels wouldn't take no for an answer. Panic stations. Imagine this under the roasting sun, with a girl you'd known less than a year, a sore head and no toilet available. I was trying desperately to hold it in but soon realised this wasn't going to work. It was shit or bust. So I jumped overboard and emptied myself into the sea. There was shite everywhere. As if that wasn't enough, I then noticed people in another boat who were out spotting dolphins. Mortified, I ducked my head under water until they went by, nearly drowning myself in the process. I tell this story in my stand-up comedy show. It was the first story I put up on my Facebook page just to test the waters, so to speak. I hit the send key while sitting in my kitchen and saying to myself, *It takes about four to five minutes to read that story, if nobody gives me feedback within ten minutes I'm deleting it.* I remember sitting there with my heart racing. I was going for it. Putting myself out there. Which is a difficult thing for anyone to do.

Next thing the silence is broken.

Ding. Ding. Ding. Ding.

I look at all these likes and notifications popping up. And I think with a mixture of relief and exhilaration: *They find this funny.*

I'd loads of these stories to tell. I was such an unfortunate disaster of a chap that anything that could wrong did go wrong for me. I really enjoyed trotting out experiences like this, writing them down, even though the spelling was a trial. The main thing was that the audience seemed to enjoy it. So once a week I'd put up a fresh story. Other stuff that happened to me. Anything.

A friend of mine, Ciarán Lenehan, who was on the Meath panel, had written a series of columns for the *Sunday Independent* taking a humorous view of the GAA from a player's perspective. I thought about doing something similar but the response to my Facebook posts encouraged me to set up Rory's Stories in November as a separate page. I continued working with CPL Recruitment, but now, at 26, I had one eye elsewhere. Ciarán was very helpful when I started the regular blog. I'd say, 'Lenno, this is going to be huge.' And I'm sure he thought, *Ah you mad cunt.* He helped set up the blog and because I couldn't spell he would edit it for me as well. It went up every Monday or Friday, and this was the start of me really going for it. I remember sitting in my mam's house and saying, 'Mam, I'm going to start Rory's Stories.' She replied, 'It's a good omen because your grandfather died on this day and it's his anniversary, the 4th of November.'

In my gut I knew I was going to take off. I just knew it. We often talk about my cousin David Murphy's 21st in Tullamore in early November of that year when we were all out in the smoking area. And people were saying, 'Ah Rory, those stories on Facebook are priceless. I've shared them and my friends are saying they're gas.' I said, 'You know, boys, I'm going to go for this comedy.' And they said, 'I'd go and see your show.' And I swear to god now I went back into the pub and I ordered a pint of Guinness and I already felt I'd made it. It's hard to explain. I just felt, *this is it, Rory, this is your calling.* And I hadn't done anything. I can't describe the feeling I had. It was as if I was already at the top table of comedy.

I remembered those times when my mam was giving out over the years, when I was drifting, and thinking somehow that there was something in there, within me, waiting to spring. I knew in amongst all those different jobs that I had something to offer that those jobs couldn't give me.

The usual drill in those early days was that I'd send Lenno a story and he'd edit it for me, before it went online. Anyone and everyone I knew who had over 500 followers on Twitter I plagued them to share my stories. Pestered them. Joe Sheridan. Kevin Reilly. Mark Ward. Dean Rock. Philly McMahon. Johnny Magee. Anyone I knew who was in the GAA circle I tortured. All these lads shared them for me. Lenno was the same, spreading the word.

I put so much work into it. I'd spend two hours on a laptop tweeting anyone with a big following. *Read this story. Read this story. Read this story.* And if I sent out 100 tweets I might get two responses but I just kept going. I was obsessed.

And just like that, I forgot about gambling.

January 2014 was the start of a new episode. That was my big year, when Rory's Stories started to take off.

I was really just being myself. Like there was a time in office jobs where I was trying to be what I might call *normal*. It wasn't me. I wanted to release that inner madness, not to suppress it. When I started doing videos in January 2014 people probably questioned my sanity. Some were mad: running after horses in fields, for example. And even in the GAA clubs, when I started doing gigs, when I was in character, I'd say whatever came into my head. I was back in the classroom, where I just slagged people and had the craic. Only this time I was doing it for a living.

Another person I hassled for publicity was Paddy Houlihan from *Mrs Brown's Boys*. I would have kind of grown up with Paddy; he's a few years older than me. Paddy and Danny O'Carroll, Brendan's son, went to school in Ashbourne and I knew them from playing street hockey games in the '90s. We had estates playing against each other and I would have played against Deerpark, who had Danny and Paddy on their side. So we went back a bit.

I spent a good amount of time on Paddy's back, trying to get my name and work more widely read. I actually think I got *Mrs Brown's Boys* to retweet my blogs once, which was massive at the time. There was another page called GAA Big Hits, run by a guy called Ruairi McCloy from Derry. I messaged him and he shared some of it as well, he was a big help. I actually did a gig in his club a few years later. You never forget people who helped you. If people ask me a favour now I'll do anything I can to help them. I can't be sharing everything on Facebook, but if there is a good luck message needed I'll do it no problem, because not that long ago I was begging people to help *me*.

Writing the blogs was enjoyable and natural, the stories flowed and it never felt like a chore. I'd finish one and then look at the reaction, the clicks, and I could be getting 200 or 300 views a week, even up to 500. I'd send my blog to my Facebook friends, people who I knew had a bit of craic in them. I'm sure they were thinking, *Would you ever fuck off and stop annoying me, Rory*. But you just got to do what you have to do. Each blog ran to around 1,000 words. And Lenno was a huge help. I'll never forget what he did for me. And at Vicar Street in 2019, the pinnacle of my career, he was definitely on the guest list.

My only previous public exposure was when Trevor O'Neill was doing comedy sketches around Ashbourne as part of a series called 'Drama Town' in 2013. He asked me to make a guest appearance: 'Do you want to play a character in a skit?' So I did and really enjoyed it. I got a real buzz out of that. The show went out in a local hotel in the autumn.

And then the videos began, which really raised my profile and proved extremely popular. At the start of 2014 I was playing with this idea of doing a sketch of a manager coming into a dressing-room prepping the players at half time in a county final. I didn't really have a script. I just had it in my head what a manager might say. I firmly believe that the funniest comedy is improvised. That's a passionate belief of mine. You come out with the funniest stuff when you're put on the spot. Like, I wouldn't be great at writing jokes but when it comes to storytelling and adding in a bit of improvisation, that's what I'm good at. That's half the battle with comedy. I used to think comedy was a man telling how two men came into a pub and there's a punchline but it's far from it. The best comedians are storytellers, telling stories you can relate to.

I had plenty of raw material right on my doorstep. One Sunday morning after training I asked the lads if they would mind taking up positions in the changing room so that I would come in playing this demented manager who would basically lash them out of it. And they went, 'Rory, are you off your head?' I said, 'I know, boys, trust me.' In fairness they all helped. I threw in the jerseys. Trevor O'Neill came down to record it and stood in the corner. I just came in and let fly, started cursing and blinding.

'Jesus Mikey get your finger out yer hole and start moving – we're five points down and we've been doing nothing. If we win this championship I promise we'll go on the beer for a week, it'll be the best craic ever.' All this kind of malarkey. So anyway, I thought it was funny enough. The next day I put that up online, on Rory's Stories, the new Facebook page. A few friends shared it. Before I knew it, Joe.ie and Balls.ie had shared it as a video.

Nobody has ever really done GAA skits in depth before. Dermot Morgan and Pat Shortt dabbled in it. But nobody had gone into the more intimate details. And I felt there was no man better than me because GAA was everything to me growing up and I knew all the characters and I felt I had a funny way of portraying things.

After I made that sketch in the dressing room, the penny dropped: I looked at this as the way to get my name out there. The GAA is at the core of Irish communities both at home and abroad; it's just a perfect platform. And just like that, I started making videos of the GAA.

Of course, the first video lacks polish and is rough around the edges. You can see a few of the lads trying not to laugh. I don't blame them. I had this mad hat on me that I got off a good friend of mine, Timmy O'Regan. Timmy was a selector for a lot of the time I played and a great footballer in his day with a sweet left peg. So I had Timmy's hat and I made sure the socks were pulled up. Because the funnier you are to look at the more people will laugh. And a thick pair of glasses to finish it off. I just had a pure and utter rural Ireland junior B manager head on me.

Paddy Murphy – young Paddy as I call him – became a key player and back-up man in the early stages of my stand-up career. Paddy played a prominent role in many of the videos: he came up with the Cecil the Cavan man character and played him. Paddy's home and my mam and dad's house are 50 yards apart. He came over one day and said he was interested in helping me with the videos. That's how it started.

Paddy was a budding actor himself who'd appeared in a few plays. He had a hunger for it. He is ten years younger than me but I needed help and was glad of it. But he knew nothing about the GAA. He played a bit but he was a Monaghan supporter because his parents were Monaghan people. And that's about as much as he knew.

There were a few other lads who helped out, like Stephen Breslin and Anthony McElearney. Pretty much the routine was that we went down every Saturday and filmed three sketches. They included the cocky corner forward, the dirty corner back, the lad who's always injured, the mad mother on the sideline, the old-school referee – anything with a GAA angle. We were filming three a day on my iPhone 4. I knew nothing about production. We'd shoot the three sketches and I'd edit them roughly on my phone. Then I'd put them up during the week.

When I started making the videos, Ciarán Lenehan, Sam Murray, my cousin Gavin Sheil, Colm Ó Méalóid and Cormac McGill were reliable advisers whose opinions I valued. They would seldom say that a video wasn't great, maybe for the sake of my confidence, but I knew they wouldn't put me wrong. I also knew what I was talking about. I played the GAA my whole life. This was ground I knew only too well.

Within six months I had 100,000 followers. It blew up. People loved it.

But for the first few weeks and months it was steady rather than spectacular. I remember when we got to around 2,000 followers we were training in Ashbourne and while we were stretching Bryan Menton, the current Meath captain, said, 'Well Rory, how many likes have you on the oul page?'

I said, 'Jeez, Mento, I just hit 2,000.' He went, 'Jeez, fair fucks, that's good going. Keep her lit like.' We laugh about it now. Remember the time I had 2,000? Now it's 550,000. Getting up to about 10,000 was the hard part, but once it hit that point it began to accelerate. I was getting 1,000 new followers a day.

I'd wake up in the morning, turn on my phone and scroll down to find another thousand. And just like that Gerry Cooney's words came back to me and I realised that my void, the one left by gambling, was being filled.

Funny the way things work out. In 2013 I had a cornea transplant. The sight in my right eye had almost completely gone and I was told I would never play football again. I remember, after the operation, leaving the Mater Hospital in bits, thinking that was the end of my GAA life.

I found out because I went for an eye test a few years back, when I was 20. The optician asked me to cover my left eye and read the lines on the chart. I couldn't see a thing. From there I was referred to an eye specialist who designed a hard lens for my right eye. My cornea was sagging, and the lens would prop it up so that I could see properly. But it was very irritating and I wasn't allowed wear the lens playing football in case I lost it. I think it cost almost €200 and I lost two or three of them before I gave up on them.

I was at the senior county final in 2006 and rooting for Wolfe Tones against the strong favourites Navan O'Mahonys – everyone loves the underdog. Cian Ward scored an unbelievable goal after which I jumped up in the air and when I sat down I realised that my lens had popped out. And my dad and I spent the next five minutes on our knees trying to find this tiny disc. I carried on for a few years without one until I decided to have the operation.

By the time of the operation I had about ten per cent sight left on that side. And this was affecting my football, obviously. You'd be calling for kick-outs and dropping balls. I used to stand in the middle of the field and cover my left eye and I couldn't see anything, I couldn't even see the goals, nothing but a blue and green haze. That also contributed to my depression.

I had to take 2014 out of football. There were stitches left in my eye. Paul Clarke, the Dublin selector and former player, took our team that year. As the year went on, I trained a bit with the lads: I'd do all the running with them so I was still part of the panel but I couldn't partake in any contact. I wanted to; I even wore a pair of special goggles. But the risks were too serious.

So the timing worked out, because without the operation and enforced absence afterwards, I wouldn't have had the time to develop Rory's Stories. When the lads were training, I would get three or four subs out to a corner and film a video. It was no surprise that Clarkey approached me and said, 'Listen, Rory, I love what you're doing and the best of luck to you but you can't be doing it on my time.' And I respected Clarkey. I knew in fairness he was right. He was trying to train a team and he'd look around for lads and I have them up the other end of the pitch shooting a video.

So while football suffered due to the operation – when we reached the county final that year I was a water-carrier – my devotion and commitment to Rory's Stories was deepening. I was still working in CPL but my mind was distracted. I was thinking of ideas, messaging people. It completely filled my time. I became very close to Paddy. We would talk a lot, exchanging ideas. Paddy would have come to a lot of the early GAA shows and we'd always have great chats coming home. We both believed that everything in life happens for a reason. We talked a lot of the time when I was seven or eight and I was best friends with Paddy's brother Kevin. Kevin got hit by a car up in Castleblayney and killed stone dead. At eight years of age. I cried my eyes out at his funeral. I still remember him in the coffin. And here 20 years later, his younger brother comes to my doorstep looking to help me.

I had a growing sense of destiny. It was as if until then I was swaying, moving all over the shop, and now I'd found a clear line. I knew exactly where I wanted to be. It was as if the only way was up. *You've been through what you're not good at. You've hung in there. You haven't given up. You've nothing to lose. How much do you want this?* When I was there begging people for help, annoying them, I was like a man possessed.

It was that addictive personality on the positive platform.

I'm going for this. I'm not taking no for an answer. I'm ready for it.

I had a great chat with Paddy Houlihan about the move I was preparing to make. He said to keep doing what I was doing, and be ready for negativity. He gave me a great bit of advice.

He said: 'If you walk into a room and there's ten in that room and four people hate you and six people love you, you're winning – always remember that.'

And I took that advice. He said no matter what you do, you're going to be criticised and abused. He said *Mrs Brown's Boys*, on paper, is one of the most successful comedy sitcoms of all time. But the number of people who hate *Mrs Brown's Boys* is unbelievable.

He added, 'Trust your gut feeling and believe in the stuff you're doing.'

And he was right. I have a lot of people who don't like what I do but I have a hell of a lot of people who do. And you need to concentrate on those people, that's the key.

What I found out quickly was that, if you're not making much noise, nobody gives a shit. When I had a few hundred likes on the Facebook page I didn't have any negative comments. I was at the stage where it was, *Oh, fair play to you for giving it a lash, respect, you're putting yourself out there, ballsy hoor.* When you have 100,000 that's when the haters come knocking. Far more people are seeing your comedy, they don't like what they see, and they throw in negative comments. When that happened, I did notice that it was generally the same names and faces, the same trolls having digs for no reason. *Cringe! This is shite!*

I ignored them. See, the human brain is designed to be negative and positive, to swing both ways. If you play a match for county or club and go into a bar after and nine people come up and say, 'Jesus, that was a great game, Rory, you really played well,' and one lad in the jacks says, 'Fuck's sake, can you not put that ball over the bar? You're useless!', who do you think about for the rest of the evening? You have to block it out as best you can. There is no human being it doesn't get to.

There are pros and cons to launching a career on social media. The upside is that it enables you to get your name out there quickly. The downside is that your haters are anonymous. In a comedy club in front of twenty people the worst that can happen is they say you're shit. Nobody messages you to say *I was at your show and you were shite.* Online they can say whatever they want, and it can be brutal. That is the most difficult part of chasing your dreams, ignoring the naysayers.

Not all the early videos were good, I know that. It was difficult when we put up a video and it started to get abuse, because we thought it was good enough. You put it out there and for whatever reason the public didn't enjoy it. And you'd read the reactions.

Ah, he's done now! Stop making videos, they're pure shite! You've had your fun. Pack it in! All this kind of stuff.

And naturally enough you're thinking, *Maybe they're right. Maybe I should quit.* And then you battle with yourself and you bust your gut again and you make another video and that goes viral. And that was the way then and it's still the way. I might put a lot of effort into making a video and it goes down like a lead balloon. Then I have a snappy topical idea, quick turnover, boom, boom, online and it goes viral.

Everyone – everyone pretty much bar my wife – thought I was nuts. I didn't listen to anyone. I was the addict on the platform and I'd go through anything to get there. I told my dad I'd be a millionaire in years to come. Out straight. *Jaysus*, he must have thought, *that lad's lost it.*

Always follow your gut. I say that in my talks to schoolkids. Your parents aren't always right. And if you are doing something that's a bit different and you feel in your stomach that it's for you, then do it. I want young people now to know that. A lot of people laughed at me when I talked of my vision.

Philly McMahon said to me years ago: 'Rory, the only thing I'll say to you is, only you have that vision. I remember having my first gym in Ballymun and three or four people there and it was costing me money to open the place. But I'd a vision.' Philly is now the owner of two thriving fitness and nutrition businesses. It's people like that you turn to for inspiration when times are hard.

I love seeing people do well. I am as far away from being a begrudger as you can get. I know how hard it is to go out there and do something different, especially in Ireland, because Ireland is a begrudger's paradise.

I've heard it all. The patronising attitudes. 'Jesus! Are you still going?' 'Well, how long more do you think you'll get out of that craic?' Fuck me, that annoys me. 'Ah, he'll get a year out of that.'

I put myself under more pressure than you'll ever imagine. But because I knew what it felt like to be outside that casino in the rain, I was ready for the challenge. The worst I could do was fail. And if I did reach 100,000 followers and then it completely died and I had to fall back on the old nine-to-five, what about it? At least I'd tried.

But I wasn't giving myself a Plan B. I had absolutely nothing to fall back on. My view is that if you have something to fall back on, you will fall back on it. Give yourself an alternative? Fuck that. Give yourself Plan A and just go at it. Like I said, I'd go to a gig and have a great gig and next thing I'd have the worst gig ever and I still had to dust myself down and go into a job that I wasn't good at, take abuse, and go back up on the Saturday and try and prove myself again. Nobody saw this. I went through the mill. In my heart and soul, I just wanted to prove to people that it could be done.

What people don't know is the ferocious determination that was in me. My mam would say, 'The thing about Rory is that if he's interested in something he'll die for you but if he's not – forget about it.' I was in uncharted territory. And I had nobody to tell me what to do. I was on my own. But was determined to go as far as I could. I was determined to make this work.

Chapter 12

On the road

LEABHARLANN CO. CHILL DARA

Filming was now taking up much of my spare time. Those Saturday excursions to the GAA club to shoot sketches consumed me, filling the headspace previously reserved for gambling. My enormous energy, which had been a lethal agent in the role of punter, was now being channelled into making videos in the GAA world where I felt most at home. I was in my element and loving every minute. It was a terrific release from the pressures that had been building up for years. What I was doing now didn't feel like work but pure pleasure. I was a man on a mission and come Saturday I was like a man possessed. If one of my assistants wasn't available I'd find someone else – the video had to be shot at all costs. Nothing could hold me back.

And I had to be resourceful. If I was shooting a video with a Galway angle, for example, I'd have to work out if Ashbourne had any Galway resident with a GAA interest. Then I'd turn up at their door. 'Can I have a loan of your Galway jersey?'

I went everywhere and anywhere looking for county jerseys to shoot in my videos when the need arose. No jersey meant no video and no video was not an option. There was no waiting until tomorrow, or another day. I continued to work without a script; instead, I'd write one or two words or phrases on a piece of paper. Little prompts. The rest was all in my head. Later I started doing shorter videos. I figured that even in this mad world, everyone has 30 seconds to watch a video.

The characters came easily since every club has one of each type. The free-taker who loves himself, who'd eat himself if he were a piece of chocolate. The guy who's always injured. The full forward who always demands the ball at the right height and in a place where he doesn't have to run too far to get it. The gym nut. The lad who trains all the time but never gets his game. They were fun to do and the positive response was a message that I was on the right track.

And the videos were the springboard to the stage. One night in Molly's Bar in Ashbourne I was asked if I'd be interested in doing a live performance. Though I had no preparation or experience, I agreed. I stood up in front of all my friends and family for about 20 minutes as part of a fundraiser for suicide awareness. And it was shite, to be honest with you. I walked off the stage thinking it had been brilliant but it definitely wasn't. I cursed way too much. That's a sign of panic, a lack of composure. In the sketch I tried to recreate the characters from the videos. Eugene. The Mad Mother. I tried to mimic Colm O'Rourke on *The Sunday*

Game. I'm not a good impressionist so that was definitely not a success. It was thrown together, frantic, chaotic. But I'd done it at least, I'd taken a step, if a small one. I never pretended to be Tommy Tiernan or had ambitions to be a stand-up comedian. I wanted to find my own way and to me this was a process of trial and error. I know people probably came to see me that night in Molly's and thought, *Ah Rory, go back to the day job!* but it was the first ever time and it's in your local pub, you know, where they don't suffer fools.

The difference between making videos and doing stand-up is, of course, that with the latter you're interacting with a live audience. You have one take. You have less control over the environment. So much more can go wrong. Really it's a whole different field even if getting laughs is still the expected end result. Through the videos I'd come to the notice of a wider GAA audience who could identify with the characters and situations being portrayed and on the back of that I started to get random invitations to do shows in GAA clubs. For some reason a lot of them were up North. I went for it. If nothing else, I needed the money, even if it wasn't going to make me rich. The takings were modest in the early days but I did it primarily because I enjoyed myself. And I'm confident I'll be a millionaire by the time I'm 40. I have no problem saying that. Because I've seen what I've done so far and how far I've come and how hard I work when I enjoy what I'm doing. Oprah Winfrey said that if you concentrate on what you're doing, money will follow you. I do believe that. If you follow your passion the rest will take care of itself.

So, in early 2014 I was still Rory O'Connor, a CPL Recruitment employee from Monday to Friday, who at the weekends turned into Rory's Stories, shooting videos and doing gigs in GAA clubs where I was as raw as they come. I was on the road, going to places I'd never been before, trusting that my brand of GAA comedy had wide reach. There was a bit of initial preparation: in advance of a show I'd email the club secretary asking him or her to identify locals who'd be a similar fit to some of my GAA characters. I might get back seven or eight names, which I'd memorise and introduce during the show and that tended to go down well. I was stepping into the unknown with no training and making loads of mistakes but I had a kind of resilience that kept me going when the shows were very much a work in progress.

In the early days I would go into a club and rant and rave, shoot from the hip, and to close I might sing two Luke Kelly songs because I'd run out of material to carry it further. This was to give the performance the impression of being longer than it really was. Sometimes they'd be happy, sometimes they wouldn't. In one club I visited in Armagh I was going around slagging people in the audience when I stopped to sit on a man's lap. I'd say he was around 70. He did not take kindly to this unrequested show of intimacy and made his frustration known by kicking me full force in the legs. For a moment I was stunned, I didn't know what to do. Obviously kicking him back wasn't an option. So I just went on as if this had never happened. At that stage I was starting to realise that this was a serious business. This was not some caper among friends down the pub. People were paying to come to see me. *Rory, you're in this for real now. No messing any more.*

Then about a couple of weeks after, I did a show in Meath that bombed and it was probably the best thing that ever happened to me. I had maybe six or seven shows under my belt when I went to Kiltale on the far side of the county. It was one of those nights where I flew through the performance, and at the end I sang a song, I think it was 'The Town I Loved So Well', which took up around six minutes and basically killed time. Blackguarding, really. I thanked the audience and walked off the stage and into the changing room. I knew straight away there was something not right. Paddy came into the changing room and we were chatting away when two ladies and a man entered, very cross-looking.

'Is it half time, Rory?' the man said.

'No, that's the show.'

'Rory, they're after paying a tenner to see you. You were only on for half an hour, that isn't good enough.'

'I'm sorry.'

They left abruptly. I think I gave them €100 back in compensation and it was the first time I felt really low doing those gigs. Not as low as the casino night in the rain, but still fairly low. The experience really jolted me. It was a wake-up call. And Paddy, even at 18, knew. We got in the car and I drove home and there wasn't a word out of me. It reminded me of one of those GAA matches you looked forward to for a long time which, come the day, just didn't go your way and on the way home you had those thoughts that you were no use. That you might as well hang up the boots. The whole way home from Kiltale that night, in my head, I was going, *Right, that's it, I'm not doing any more. That was just disgusting.* I got home and got into bed beside Emma and she asked how it had gone.

'Oh Emma that was horrible. They actually said it was way too short.'

She told me to just forget about it. And I knew I had a show the following week up in the North. All booked, tickets sold. I was only charging clubs a couple of hundred euro at the time and I could have walked away and saved myself further grief, but I could not quit. Nor did I want to. I needed to dust myself down and get on with it. So, lesson learned, I went out and bought myself a stopwatch. And I made a commitment to all future audiences: *I will not walk off that stage until I've done a minimum of 45 minutes.* I mapped out a plan, and the likely time it would take to get through each part of the show. At different intervals I'd check the watch. I'd get random people up and have them doing push-ups if I needed to. Then I started working more on the stories and built it up from there. The preparation got better, as it had to.

Kiltale in hindsight was a blessing and a boot up the hole. It showed I had to work at it and that failing to prepare, as the saying goes, is preparing to fail. You needed a contingency plan, to be ready for unforeseen events. You could get seven names from a GAA club in advance – a key part of the show – and five might not show up on the night. So you had to improvise. That's how I really learned to work off the cuff. Sometimes it went really badly, sometimes I could get really lucky. I was always glad to have a headbanger in the crowd who would go off slagging me, I'd be happy to let him have the stage.

You keep talking pal, this clock is ticking away.

Gradually the show stretched into an hour of content. There were lots of trip-ups. But the bottom line was that I wasn't afraid to fail. I flopped numerous times, often coming home on that M1, having been up the North, wondering, *Oh god, what the fuck am I doing here?*

I remember doing a gig, I can't remember the club, you were meant to start at nine and everyone at that time was still upstairs drinking in the bar. They were asked to make their way down for the start of the show. But clearly they were in no rush. In those days I was a man of simple means. I didn't carry any gear or equipment – all I needed was a mic for the room. But that venue had a massive stage, for starters, and the mic had a really short lead, so that meant there could be no mingling with the audience, reducing my options. Come showtime there were around a hundred mostly empty chairs before me, the patrons virtually handcuffing themselves to the bar, by now having moved to the downstairs bar in the function room where I was waiting to start. The drinkers were refusing to budge.

'Right, lads, take your seats!'

Hardly anyone moved. I looked at Paddy and he said, 'I don't know either, Rory, you might as well just start.'

That hour I spent more or less talking to myself. I remember going up at one point and trying to hoosh them down from the bar but they wouldn't come. And for an hour I just died on my hole. And I'm sure if you spoke to anyone present that night they'd say, 'I went to see that guy Rory's Stories and my god he's brutal.'

I expected the club to shut the bar and at least give me a bit more consideration and respect but this was a night they wanted to make money and the bar was hopping. I had helped bring in the customers so that was probably my job done, but it didn't do much for my confidence. Then I'd drive back down home pissed off with myself, raging that I got into this, and then I'd have to get up on Monday and go to that office job.

I was doing roughly one gig every weekend. Armagh and Down were probably the most regular destinations. I seemed to go down well in those counties and I reckon I did around ten clubs around Newry alone over a couple of years. Some nights you'd get there and there would be 30 people present and it'd be absolutely horrendous. Sometimes you could have 300 or 400, the place jammed. When there were that many people I often wondered how I'd get through it, still being a fairly raw act, though gradually that changed to the point where bigger crowds increased my confidence rather than diminished it.

I also did those gigs because I felt that I had to. I needed the few bob, to be honest about it. We were renting a house and had a young child. I wasn't on a great wage in work. Every one good gig was worth two bad ones. The high of people laughing their heads off and thinking you're hilarious, coming up to you afterwards and going, 'Jesus, Rory, that was priceless' – that made the pain manageable when it didn't go well. And what I loved was that people took the gamble to have me there. You'd have old-school lads in the club wondering, I'm sure, *Why're we getting this guy? Never heard of him.* But I could strike a chord with enough people out there to make it work, to pull in an audience.

On nights where those clubs would sell their couple of hundred tickets, and I'd put on a good show, I'd feel great because they took the risk and it paid off. I'd be delighted for them. And if it was a bad show I felt guilty for the same reason. But overall, I really enjoyed the trips. I carried the shows through into 2015 and worked on them, but for a few years after there were still nights where you walked off the stage relieved the torture was over. The stage can be a lonely place.

I had to keep believing, no matter what others thought. I remember one day in 2014 or maybe 2015 leaving the house and Emma asked where I was going. I said, 'I'm going to make videos.' She goes, 'Oh, you and those stupid videos.'

And I'm saying, 'I'm telling you now, them videos are going to make us a lot of money in a few years' time.' She's like, 'Yeah, but they're not making any money now, are they?'

And I slammed that door and got into the car and it was one of those moments when I told myself that no matter what, I'm going to make this work. I often remind her of this. I did a show in Toronto in 2019, and I brought Emma over with me, we had four days there, lovely hotels, lovely meals, and I kept saying to her, 'Now, what about that time you said …' I love bringing that up. I was pig-determined.

In 2015, my last year of part-time touring, I was invited to do a gig in Boston along with the former Meath footballer Joe Sheridan. The invitation came through another former Meath footballer, Charles McCarthy, who was living in Boston and involved with a local club. He asked if I would be interested in taking part in this Rose of Tralee spoof, where I would be the presenter and Joe, dressed up as a woman, would be a competitor.

I don't think it was a huge amount of money but anything that came my way I was happy to take, especially one like this. I was still working in CPL and an opportunity to go to Boston, I think it was for four nights, was too good to turn down. It would also be good for my profile. I would have known Joe already through football. I suppose who doesn't know Joe after the 2010 Leinster final? When I was playing minor for the club at 15 he was playing at the same grade for Seneschalstown, a powerful full forward, unstoppable. His brother Damien played midfield and I also came up against him a few times on the club circuit – a tough cookie. And there was also another brother, Brian, who played centre forward, maybe the best footballer of the lot of them, skill-wise. Whenever you played Seneschalstown, if you kept the Sheridans quiet you generally won.

So Joe and I took the plane to Boston, both welcoming the chance to let off some steam. The first night over there we went out for a few drinks but I knocked off a bit earlier because the gig was on the following night. It was run by the Wolfe Tones club and around 400–500 people turned up. I was nervous and winging it but it went down well. Once I put away the mic and the show was over I could relax. We had a good night and the next day after the breakfast we went straight to The Banshee, which is a popular Irish sports bar in Boston, where there was a free tab and plenty of craic. We spent much of the day just enjoying the company and sharing stories.

We did a full day in The Banshee and then Charles offered to take us to this late bar and nightclub on the far side of town. The three of us hopped into a taxi and headed there. Around 4 a.m. Charles went home. Joe and I had one more drink and realised we were starving so we left the night club to go looking for food. We were wandering around when, suddenly, to our delight, we spotted a Chinese restaurant in the distance. But as we neared the place looked strange, like there was something not quite right. There was a Ferrari parked outside for a start, and a gang of maybe five lads hanging about with a kind of gangster look about them. They seemed surprised when we ordered food.

We waited for the food and when it arrived, ate quickly and left. Then we sprinted down the road as fast as we could go, Chinese food and a load of drink sloshing about in our systems. We turned down an alley and in our paranoia, vowed to each other we'd fight if we had to. Just then a taxi man pulled up.

'Get the fuck in, what are you doing here?'

We didn't need a second invitation. The driver explained that this was an unsafe area and we were taking a big risk being there. Two big gormless Meath lads at that hour of the morning were like target signs. We might as well be carrying placards saying SHOOT ME. The restaurant was, I think, being used for laundering cash. It was a relief to get out of there in one piece and when we arrived back in the hotel we had another a drink to settle the nerves. There at the bar we both considered what might have happened if the taxi man hadn't arrived like a knight in shining armour. We could have met a bad end. All for the sake of a feed.

The videos became so popular that by 2015 I was regularly being stopped for photos. I got to experience a kind of celebrity status, which I found strange. Going up North on a Saturday I might have to do 50 or 100 selfies with people after the gig. And then after this big show I would get back into my 05 Volkswagen Polo with the petrol cap missing. I was fortunate to have it. The car had belonged to my late and much-loved granny Bee and was handed down to me free of charge. But I used to park it a bit away from the GAA clubs because I didn't want people to see the kind of car I was driving. The one time the lads spotted me in the Polo I had to let on it was the girlfriend's car and my own jeep was in the garage.

Before I went full-time it was like I was living a double life. I was slightly famous at the weekend and then back in the office job during the week, being hauled over the coals over some spreadsheets; no one knew about my work on Rory's Stories. I just got on with it and never mentioned it unless someone else did. Like, we dealt with people from the North and a lad rang me one day and said, 'Are you really Rory's Stories?' I confessed, and he went, '[Northern accent] Holy fuck boy, I love you, what are you doing in this job?' I said, 'I'm actually working here for 28 grand a year.'

That split was a little weird. Even if I was out in the likes of Copper Face Jacks, there were people getting photos taken with me. I was still playing football with the lads, but even on the football field I'd started to get a bit more attention. We played a friendly one day and I was late into a tackle and hit a fella and he goes, 'Oh, you think you're great now because you're a celebrity.'

Another time we were playing a game where there was a bit of a melee, and a fella hit one of our lads and I came in and took our lad away, as you would, protecting him, and a lad came in and half-jostled me and says, 'You're not on fucking Facebook now, boy!' And like everyone on the sideline heard it and started laughing. It was funny. And even after matches with the intermediate team, young lads coming up looking for photos after the game with me. It was all a fairly surreal experience. I suppose I was adapting to becoming a more public figure.

People ask me if it doesn't wreck my head getting asked for photos when I'm out with Emma. There's times when it does but overall it's grand. That's because I was given great life lessons as a young lad.

For example, when I was 16 my dad brought me to see a famous band. I was a huge fan of theirs and it was unusual of someone of my age to be a fan of this group back then. They were playing in Ashbourne House and we were hanging around in the lobby when their lead singer walked by and my dad says, 'Rory, go over and ask him for his autograph.' I sidled over. Asked for the autograph. 'I'm busy,' he grunted and kind of brushed past me, leaving me standing with an empty piece of paper. And I was thinking to myself, *What a prick!*

And, you know, years later, a lot of young people would be asking me for photographs and I'd embrace every one of them because I know that all it takes is ten seconds. You take a photo with this young lad that he might remember for the rest of his life and think to himself, *Oh I met Rory's Stories and he's a nice fella.* I learned from that experience when I was 16. The guy in question didn't realise that ten seconds of his time was all I needed to think well of him. So now if I'm eating in a restaurant and a young fella comes over and asks for a selfie, and I have my wife with me and a chicken wing in my mouth, it might not be ideal but I'll say, 'Yeah, give me one second there.' And if catch myself thinking, *Ah do you mind? Not now!* I immediately remind myself of the time I was his age and someone I looked up to walked away and made me feel small.

I'm more used to people looking at me when I'm out now. I will talk to anyone and Rory's Stories will never, ever change me from being the person I am. If you're a prick and you're given money and fame, you become a bigger prick. If you're a nice fella and you become famous you become a nicer fella. I believe that.

Early in 2016 Dave Anderson came on board as my agent, which opened up new commercial and revenue streams. That was another sign that this was serious, there was no turning back. Cian Twomey, who would have been a huge Facebook hit for a few years, had Dave as his manager and it was he who recommended him when we were talking one day. I knew I needed to take this to the next level. I'd done a few promotional videos that earned some money here and there but I felt I needed a more professional approach. I was looking for someone to guide me in the right direction. So I met Dave for a coffee.

Dave was a real Southside Dubliner: posh kind of a fella, smart, well-reared, college-educated and all that kind of stuff. And here sitting opposite him was this GAA, LCA head. I said, 'Listen, I'm a very honest man, and I expect you to be the same, so if you fuck me over, I swear to god, I'll break your nose.' I wasn't trying to be the hard man. I was just letting him know that I'd heard some bad stories about agents and that I'm basically a fella that could be easily codded and that I don't know any other reaction than to go for you if you mess with me. And I told him that, straight up. And he was a bit taken aback. We've laughed about it ever since. Dave was a key man in progressing my career after I'd paddled through 2015 by myself.

He didn't get involved in the shows – I continued to look after that side – but he went out seeking work for me in other areas like advertising and promoting brands. We hit it off from the beginning. I did a college gig in early 2016 that he came along to watch. He liked what he saw and thought there would be a bit of a niche in the market for me. Along with Mark Jacobs he runs the Outset agency, which has been going from strength to strength in recent years: when I started working with them they had three or four employees, now they're up to ten or so. I speak to Dave as much as I speak to my wife. We've built up a brilliant relationship and I consider him a close friend now. Dave and Mark were at my wedding. I trust Dave: he's a genuinely good fella and a hard worker. I definitely don't think my career would be where it is without his guidance.

His nose is safe, for now.

Chapter 13

Going back down under

I went full time with Rory's Stories in January 2016. I'd got a bit of redundancy off CPL when I finished up the previous September, which covered the bills for maybe three or four months. So I worked out the maths: I had four months or so of going to these GAA clubs to keep me tipping over. CPL were downsizing and offered voluntary redundancy and I was advised that it would be a wise course to avail of it, that the job might not be there much longer if I remained on. I spoke to Emma about going out on my own and we discussed what we needed to get by. She figured I needed about €22k a year to live with a small degree of comfort.

After I left CPL and before I went out fully on my own I took a job as a salesman selling this little box device that carried advertisements and promotions on pub television screens. The company that made them was trading on my name, because I had already built up a bit of a profile through the videos and shows. I'd go into these bars and talk shite. But in truth I didn't know an awful lot about the product and the company went bust within three months. In early January 2016 we were all called in and told the news.

I think they were paying me €30k a year without commission. I never sold a thing. But the travel was enjoyable. I drove around a good few pubs in Leinster as I was the rep for the province. I would have gone to Drogheda one day, taken in every pub in the town. Newbridge another day. Naas. Portlaoise. And just talked nonsense. Now not all of them would know me but a good few did. They'd chat away but still have no interest in buying. A salesman needs to be confident about the product he's selling but sure I didn't even know what that thing did, the training we had was so poor. I was like a cowboy going around with this yoke. And like it was one box per telly, which made no sense. I remember being in a busy bar in Drogheda and yer man was like, 'I presume this box will be connected to all the tellies?' And I was going, 'Erm, yeah, yeah, erm yeah, I'm sure, of course it does, yeah.' And I rang the manager that night and he goes, 'No, Rory, you need a box per telly, but tell him we can do him a discount.'

And when your man called us in and broke the news in January, I felt now was the time to go for it. I knew it was a risk, going full time, but my heart was telling me to plough on. I went back to that feeling I had at David Murphy's 21st. *Look at what you've achieved already*, I thought. I had a quarter of a million followers at that stage. I was getting better in the GAA clubs, my act was becoming more polished, and Dave was coming on board as my agent, which would guarantee more revenue. So, I said to myself, *Fuck it, why not?*

Even though things are going well I worry about being self-employed – especially now, writing this book during the global pandemic. But rather than looking too far ahead, I look at how far I've come. Jim Carrey has a good outlook on this. He said people need to stop worrying about the future because all we'll ever have is the here and now. Stop worrying about tomorrow and take today as it comes. And tomorrow you can worry about tomorrow. Conor McGregor – though I admit he's not everyone's cup of tea – is also someone I admire for his persistence and self-belief. I take inspiration from anyone who takes a chance, who works hard in what they believe in.

Eventually I started to broaden the range of material beyond the GAA world and began including material more people might be familiar with, like lads on building sites and family scenarios. And that was where Enya Martin came in. We teamed up on videos, doing joint ventures, and that widened the audience. The videos we did as a couple became hugely popular. Part of the reason for that was that we had a good rapport and connection – in fact people often think we're a real couple.

I'd seen a few of Enya's videos and had an idea of making videos involving couples in typical domestic scenes. I could see there was a lot of potential there. I rang Enya, introduced myself, invited her for a coffee. Presented the idea. Enya wasn't driving at the time so I went over to Neilstown, where she lives. The chemistry seemed to work and the videos started to go viral. They were getting a couple of million views every week. Big hitters.

That's when I noticed it going to another level. I was used to at this stage going into matches at Croke Park and getting noticed but now because we were doing these couples sketches it moved on to a different dimension. And it was a welcome change for me as I think I had almost bled the GAA dry; I'd exhausted all the characters. I wanted to prove that I wasn't a one-trick pony.

The videos with Enya just seemed to click with people. We'd shoot a sketch of a couple having an argument and in ten minutes it would have had 20,000 views. Boom. We came up with ideas together. We weren't writing scripts as such, but creating scenarios. She knew what to say, the two of us bounced off each other. Paddy would often record it. She'd nail it every time. It was almost telepathic. Usually the response I'd have in my head she'd deliver it. Enya and I worked together for about two years. They were familiar scenarios: a couple planning the wedding list. A couple going on a diet. A couple going for a drink. I drew from everywhere I could think of.

I started to draw on my own childhood and my youth more too. Those trips I loved as a child to Offaly, to the farm my father was brought up on, became particularly useful fodder. Those were great adventures for a boy coming out of an estate in Ashbourne. I drove the tractor with my Uncle

Finn, who's also my godfather. I worked on the bog. As a townie I wasn't used to a day's work like that, footing and turning turf by hand. I recalled days when I had to man a gap while the uncle was moving cattle when I was maybe nine or ten. I'd be waiting for the cattle to pass and nervous as fuck in case they got through, and when they were near I'd have a sudden rush of confidence and slap the last one on the arse with a hurl or whatever I was holding, as much to say, 'There's the last of them there now, Finn.' All of this I translated into comedy that people could recognise and enjoy.

In September 2016 Rory's Stories received an invitation to travel to Australia for the Australasian Gaelic Games Championships in Brisbane. This was a major event involving a broad sweep of GAA teams from all over Australia and New Zealand and I was being flown out to MC the awards that were being presented at its culmination. By any measure it was a huge gig and one that I could not let pass.

Partly responsible for this was a good friend, a guy called Padraig Finn, otherwise known as 'Sharkey'. I'd played football with him for years before he settled over there. He made contact with Dave, my manager, and between them they combed through the finer details. Dave and I agreed that I should do some other work while I was there to make the most of the opportunity.

So we made contact with the Clann na Gael GAA club in Sydney to see if they were interested in the show and they agreed to host it in the famous Cock 'n' Bull bar in Sydney's Bondi Junction. And while I was in Brisbane for the main event, we arranged to do another show in O'Malley's pub.

I went out on a bit of a wing and a prayer. To be honest, I wasn't ready. My main experience was drawn from various GAA clubs around home, a mix of good and bad nights. But, as the old saying goes, there's never a perfect time for anything. I wasn't in a position to say, 'Listen, would you give us a couple of years there and let me come back when I've a bit more material?' No, I decided. *You just have to do this, Rory.*

I was looking forward to a new challenge, but travelling solo was a bit lonesome. It's a long haul at the best of times but particularly by yourself, and I was leaving Ella and Emma for three weeks. But it was something I needed to do, and I was being paid well. I had to consider that also. Off I headed on a long journey to Brisbane on the other side of the world. At least I knew that Sharkey was waiting for me (he was attached to a GAA club in Brisbane). He was my safety net.

I hadn't seen Sharkey in a while and sure we went on the beer when I landed, jetlag or no jetlag. The games were under way so I would go down to the venues and show my face. It was weird enough because I was a kind of celebrity there and I wasn't used to that. It was funny having everyone looking at me. I felt like saying, with a big megaphone, 'Please, don't treat me any differently. I am actually normal. I am no different from anyone else.' They would have been used to seeing this fella on Facebook and YouTube and now he was amongst them in the flesh. So I was standing there, big dopey sunburnt head on me watching the games. But I loved when people came up to me to chat and naturally there were a few from Meath, some of whom I would have known or played against over the years.

My first gig was on in O'Malley's. And it was absolutely shite. The audience probably numbered about 20. And between that and me not having too much material prepared, deciding I would just try to have the craic with people in the room, it fell flat on its face. I'm sure the person who booked me was pretty disappointed. Because O'Malley's was one of the tournament sponsors, the small crowd came as a surprise to me, but Sharkey explained that a lot of the visitors would have been on drink bans. Teams took this seriously. They came to Brisbane to win the titles. Like, the standard was pretty good. Three or four days of games, football and hurling and ladies' football and camogie. What I loved, watching the football matches, was that every kick-out went out to the middle of the field. It was too hot for this short kick-out nonsense so there was a lot of high fielding. The ball would be put down on the tee and lumped out the field for the players to contest in the air like football used to be played. That was great to see.

So we got through the night in O'Malley's, Sharkey was there with me, and he knew it wasn't a great success. 'Ah, you know yourself, Rory, you've plenty to learn.' He'd be honest enough. It wasn't a professional show by any means.

It was just a lad telling the odd story and having a bit of fun with the crowd. I did a few characters but I couldn't improvise like at home because I didn't have any names to play with. I didn't beat myself up over it. I thought, *Rory, you're only learning. You know yourself. You're definitely way out of your comfort zone here. Enjoy it for what it is and don't be afraid to fail.* And that attitude kept me going. I did the gig and, like I said, not a great one at all but I got through to the other side. What about it? Move on.

If I had a bad gig I'd often say to myself, *Hey, listen, you could be on that 103 bus back into that office job. Snap out of it.* I always put it into context, and reminded myself that stress in this environment was good stress compared to stress in an office where I was in a job that I had no passion for. My dad used to ask me: is it the same stress as you experienced in CPL or other jobs? And I would say, absolutely not. And to be honest, whenever I had a bad gig, another thing I might say to myself was, *You could be dead in the morning, Rory, nobody really gives a fuck.* And that's another attitude I always carry. A lot of it is in your own head. It's like playing football. You might play great and by the time you drive home you feel you had the worst game in your life. That's the self-doubt preying on the brain.

I was only at the comedy two years. And to be flown to Australia to do those gigs was probably ahead of the curve. You often hear that it takes ten years for a comedian to find his footing. I had to reassure myself, *Rory, you're only two years at it. You have to learn.* I knew I was funny, that I had a talent and passion for comedy and storytelling, but I was still learning, sometimes the hard way. I was working towards a time when I would be able to deliver my show more reliably and consistently. Towards a day when I'd leave nothing in the dressing room, to use a favourite GAA pep-talk expression.

With O'Malley's over, we came to the main awards night. I had a simple job: present a few prizes and do a bit of comedy for maybe 15 minutes. I was told by one of the organisers that there would be a few old-school types present and not to be too extreme or graphic. To moderate the act a little. But Sharkey, being Sharkey, said to hell with that, advising me to throw caution to the wind. 'Rory, slate them, who gives a fuck, that's what people want to hear, some slagging.' I erred on the side of caution. I had a few jokes I held back, which might have offended more delicate members of the audience. I'd say I went 60 per cent of the way. After the awards, feeling I'd hit the right notes and it had gone down well, I went into the toilet. I was having a piss and there was a fella beside me, and he says, 'Oh, how are you Rory, yeah good night.' And he walked out. And in comes this other man in his I'd say early 60s, a small butty fella, who goes, 'You should be ashamed of yourself!' And I said, 'Excuse me?' And he went, 'We flew you over here and all you've done is abuse people, I hope you have someone to walk you home tonight.' He threatened me, like.

I was trying to take all this in. My natural impulse was to say, 'Who the fuck do you think you are?' And basically go for him. But it was one of the first times in my life I had to realise that I'm not Rory O'Connor, I'm Rory's Stories. I have a reputation to protect. I have some added responsibility. So I took a deep breath and let the moment pass.

And I wouldn't mind but this lad was up to my fucking nipple – a 60-year-old man! Even the thought of throwing a dig would knock him out. And I was thinking, *what is this lad's problem?* So I said, 'Whatever, get out of my sight.' And he left anyway. I went out to one of the organisers and explained what had happened, told her I was after being abused, and she went, 'Don't mind him, he's part of the old school, people who didn't want to bring you over for this. He has a chip on his shoulder. Take no offence from him.'

I was the special guest for the evening. I didn't hand out all the awards, I handed out a few. And maybe ten minutes of improvised humour, but obviously that was enough to piss off this dinosaur. It was another lesson, that you need to show restraint. You can't say what you want to say, you certainly can't get physical with this kind of fella. You have to ignore them. Which can be difficult. If it was a few years before that I am sure there would have been a row in the toilet. I knew all it needed was me grabbing him by the neck and he running out crying assault and that's me, Rory's Stories, finished.

Anyway, the night went on and we'd a great time and the next day we went on the beer in Brisbane. The craic was great but the following day Sharkey drove me to the airport to fly on to Sydney and I was feeling pretty low and exhausted. Three days of drinking was taking its toll. I was going to Sydney by myself to do a show where I heard there were 400 tickets sold. And I wasn't in any way ready for this show whatsoever. But anyway, Sharkey gave me a hug, and I headed off. Before the boarding gate opened, I ordered a pint in a bar to settle myself. My mind was racing. I was missing my family. The system was just run down from too many sessions. And then a woman came up to me and asked if anyone was sitting next to where I was. And when I said no, she sat down.

She was Australian and she told me a story about her son who wasn't well, and how she was going to visit him. It was just a really engaging story and, without her realising, she cheered me up. And it shows the impact you can have on people, even ones you don't know, if you just sit down, pull up a chair and have a chat, it can make a really positive difference. We spoke for around half an hour or so and had a couple of drinks. She was an older lady, maybe late 50s, so it wasn't that we were chatting each other up. Just having a normal conversation that both of us probably needed at the time. Then we went our separate ways, she headed off in her direction and I went on to Sydney. And we knew we would probably never see or speak with one another again. The time spent talking to this lady helped ease my anxiety and fears and put my mind more at rest.

When I landed in Sydney, I took a taxi into the city. Clan na Gael had an apartment waiting for me in Coogee Bay, which is a popular haunt for the Irish. By the time I got there it was around midnight. And by then I was fairly tired and the fear was kicking back in. All I wanted to do was go to bed and log on to the Wi-Fi and FaceTime home or something. I didn't want to interact with anyone beyond that. I was walking down Coogee Bay beachfront, nobody around, looking for my apartment's location when three lads came walking towards me. And what were the chances?

'Ah! Rory's Stories, boy!'

Three head-the-balls from Louth.

'How're ye, lads?'

'Ah Rory, come on, we're going to a house party.'

'No, no, boys, I'm grand.'

'No, come on. Oh you're a mad cunt, you're a mad hoor.'

'Ah yeah, can't, I'm sick of drink, I just want to go and lie down.'

We chatted away for a few minutes, they were sound fellas, we spoke about the 2010 Leinster final when Meath robbed Louth with Joe Sheridan's controversial goal, we had a bit of craic with that. So after they left I went up to the apartment. And just my luck – the electricity wasn't working. And I'd no contact number to ring anyone. So I couldn't connect to the Wi-Fi.

I lay there. And anyone that's been on the beer for three days will know what it's like when you cannot sleep. I was lying there, nothing happening. Just me and my thoughts, which can be very unpleasant when you've a lot of alcohol in the system. And as I lay there I sweated and I tossed and I turned. And then I'd say at about four in the morning, after three hours of twisting and turning, I'd had enough of the torment and I put on my runners and I put on my T-shirt and my shorts and I went out on to Coogee Bay and I ran up and down the beach for an hour to get rid of my anxiety till the sun came up.

And I ran up and I ran down, and I ran up and I ran down, and I puked a bit, and I ran up and down again. And then when the sun came up, I took off my clothes and wearing just the boxers I jumped straight into the sea. Floated around in the sea, came out, went back and had a shower and slept for 12 hours. I felt like a new man.

That was one of the first times I properly realised how much exercise can help when you are struggling with your mental health. I needed something to curtail those negative thoughts. Obviously, alcohol is one route. Drinking more. Looking for the cure. But that wasn't an option any more, I realised.

When I woke up I rang the fella who was my contact and he came down and we met and we'd a coffee, he sorted out the electricity in the apartment, the Wi-Fi was working again, and just like that everything else was back on track.

The gig was about two or three days away but I avoided alcohol and I had a few clear days to prepare a show. I knew I couldn't wing it anymore. So I started writing fresh material. For those two days I actually worked harder than I'd ever worked for a show. I was videoing myself telling stories in the apartment. I was thinking of Irish people abroad. I was coming up with expat angles like Skyping the mother and father and what I'd do then was I'd shoot a ten-minute video and WhatsApp it to two or three people who had lived in Australia to get their feedback. For the first time ever, I started to really think about what I was doing. And I memorised a few jokes and stories and that.

My cousin Dee and her husband Felipe were in Sydney and I went and stayed a night with them, which was great for the head as well. Felipe, he's Brazilian, cooked us a Brazilian barbecue, and we had maybe two or three beers, everything nice and relaxed. I spoke to him about my comedy and what I planned on doing. It made me feel a lot less homesick just being around them. Two of my childhood friends, Simon and Conor, were in Sydney at the time and they were coming to the show and Felipe came as well.

So I felt a lot more confident going into the Sydney gig even though it was only two days of preparation. But sure, fuck it – it was better than nothing. I wouldn't say I was as well prepared as most comedians would be for a 400-person show but I was more prepared than I usually would have been. More than just going into a club with seven names and looking anxiously at the clock all through what followed.

How did it go? It went alright, so-so. I was the first ever comedian to perform there, it being more of a band venue. It certainly wasn't intimate by any stretch of the imagination. You had me on stage, a barrier around me and a load of Irish headbangers drinking and having the craic. The material I tried about the Skyping went down well, got good laughs, and I then moved on to talk about moving to Australia and all these great intentions you have, and how you end up in certain pubs and building sites and how Irish people come all this way to get away from Ireland and yet they still find themselves in Irish bars listening to Luke Kelly. And all this kind of lark. And everyone was enjoying this.

Then I noticed the atmosphere was getting a bit rowdy, and that's when my character Eugene had to come into play so I stuck on the hat and glasses and I went for it then. That was definitely pure improvisation. I went down into the crowd and if I saw a fella talking or not enjoying himself, I just dragged him up on stage and slagged him. I was carefree and enjoying it. Compared to my show now it wasn't good at all, but from where I was at that point it was pretty decent. For the amount of time I prepared, which was two days, it was satisfactory.

The club sold about 400-odd tickets, A$25 a pop, so they were clearly happy. I ended the show by telling the audience to be proud of where they were from. I enjoyed it more than O'Malley's anyway. Afterwards myself and Conor, Simon and Felipe had a few drinks and it was great catching up with them, and they were saying, 'Jesus, we never thought you'd be here doing comedy, and us messing around the shops for years.'

I learned a lot about myself on that trip, above all that I needed to start preparing better for shows. You might wonder had I not realised that already. I kinda did. But I was still too casual at times and too dependent on being able to talk myself out of a situation. I don't know whether I was just being lazy but I kept thinking I'd be grand. I also couldn't ignore the potential for reputational damage: if standards dropped, obviously bookings would too. And there was the impact on my mental health when shows were not going well. When I left a bad gig I'd say to myself that I needed to work on more material. I had made some gradual improvements and generally gigs were going well, but I was in too much of a comfort zone.

Dave said before I went to Australia that if I wasn't ready it would be fine, don't go, but at the same time, even though really I was not ready, I felt I couldn't afford to put this on hold. And it goes back to what I often say to people: don't be afraid to jump in at the deep end. So I took a punt. This was a gamble, admittedly, but a much safer one that what had led me down a dark path in the past.

I began to realise that learning how to work the stage would not be one smooth rise to the top of the mountain but a whole series of attempts, each failed mission leaving an invaluable lesson for the next assault. This was climbing with no rope. Climbing and falling back down again and then restarting as if it was your first attempt. You had to keep dreaming. You had to think of the day you'd reach the summit and pin the flag. Come what may.

Chapter 14

New York, New York

During my first year of full-time performing I continued to tour GAA clubs and develop the show. I started to do the odd wedding where a couple were looking for a little entertainment around mealtime. That tended to be very hit and miss. You're going into a room with 200-odd people and not all of them know who you are and some don't like your comedy. I did this one wedding and literally two tables got up and walked out, as much to say, 'We're not listening to this prick.' And that can hard on your confidence. I've also done weddings where people got a great laugh and I texted the bride and groom a few days later to thank them for having me and that, and they might say you were the talk of the wedding and how it was a great highlight. Again, ups and downs.

I had more time now to devote to developing the comedy but those first few years were a steep learning curve. It could take me three days to memorise nine names at the start. That took a while to get the hang of. Whereas now you can hand me a sheet of nine names the night before a gig and I'll have them memorised no bother. When not working on the next show I'd be scrambling around making videos, which remained popular and had a wide reach, and that first year I also made a television appearance on *Republic of Telly*, much of it down to persistence. Aside from work it was also great to be at home with Ella, who was starting playschool. Being more a part of her life was a luxury I wouldn't have had before. It made life better and me a lot happier.

In March 2016 Emma and I went to Edinburgh for Paddy's weekend, where I'd been invited to do a show in a local GAA club. The tickets never sold and they decided to cancel. Naturally that's a blow, but we made the most of the trip and had a great break by turning it into a celebration of my 29th birthday. Even if there were bruising experiences along the way I never thought for a moment I'd made the wrong move. It was in Edinburgh that time I saw Ballyboden win the All-Ireland, managed by Andy McEntee, and that made my day. Nine years after leading us to an intermediate title he had reached the summit of club football. Not least because of Andy I was now in a better place in every respect, even if there were bumps on the journey.

The following year, March 2017, I was back on a plane ready for another international adventure, this time taking Rory's Stories to New York. Little did I know what lay in store. By neat coincidence the trip happened to correspond with my 30th birthday, which falls on St Patrick's Day. Monaghan had won the New York championship for the first time in an eternity, and they were flying me out as a special guest to do a skit at their dinner dance. I rang Tony. 'I'm going to New York.' He goes, 'I'm coming with you.'

Dave, as he had done the year before, started exploring other possibilities while we were out there. He came up with an offer from The Chelsea Bell, a new Manhattan bar, which was run by an Irishman. I was pencilled in for two gigs there. Again, the idea was to make my trip as worthwhile and beneficial as possible.

Tony and I hatched a plan that would suit everybody. The lads would fly out for four days to start with and the girls would join us for Paddy's Day to celebrate my 30th. So we had four days by ourselves and then a few days with the girls. I wanted Tony with me, being my best friend, and he wanted to go for the session and the craic. I often said that Tony could easily do what I do. He is one of the funniest people I know. But he'd tell you that he wouldn't dream of walking onto the stage: 'I can tell you a story that'll make you laugh but fuck me if I'm going up there with a mic.'

So we headed off to Dublin airport, giddy with excitement. And as you can imagine two lads going on the hop for four days was a chance not to be missed. We were sitting there with about a half hour to board and Tony was saying, 'Ah, I can't wait for this.' Imagine the pair of us heading to New York for St Patrick's Day, to celebrate my 30th. And I'm getting paid for the privilege. And then he says, 'Well, money won't be an obstacle this time.' And I looked over and Tony had an envelope in his hand and he must have had a couple of grand in cash stuffed inside, determined not to leave himself short while he was in the Big Apple. He says to me, 'You're only 30 once, Rory.' *He must have taken out his life's savings*, I thought to myself.

Well, we couldn't have spent it if we tried. We were treated like royalty. Everywhere we went in New York I was getting free drinks because people recognised me from Rory's Stories. Tony kept saying that he needed to get rid of the money before the women got over. But it was to prove difficult.

The Monaghan dinner dance was being staged the night after we arrived. Mindful of past experiences, once we landed, I said to Tony, 'I'm taking it handy tonight. We're not going on the beer. I have to be someway fresh for this gig tomorrow.' So we had a few drinks, nothing mad. We were staying in a hotel near Times Square.

So far, so sensible. The Monaghan dinner dance was an easy gig. For starters, those present were all in great form. And I had a few names in advance that I could work off. Tony was invited as a friend and they put on a free bar. I had to perform for just 20 minutes so there wasn't really much pressure. I produced my usual Eugene character, ripping the piss, and then at the end I spent some time presenting their awards and that was me done. Time to party.

I'd never been in New York before. But we were definitely leaving the sightseeing until the girls arrived. Our sole interest for the time being was having a good time and going on the beer. We had no interest in the Statue of Liberty or

Ground Zero, anything like that. We just wanted to make the most of the time we had because we knew when the girls landed the craic would be more curtailed. You know yourself, lads are lads.

After the gig we got sucked into a session with the Monaghan lads and ended up in the Mean Fiddler, which is like the Coppers of New York, a famous Big Apple institution. All the Irish go there. We had a great session that night, with the work out of the way, mixing with all these Irish people just before Paddy's Day. The manager there was a fella called Donal ('Ducky') Kelly from Ashbourne who looked after us. It was a promising start and we made it back to the hotel in the early hours happy that the evening had gone well and knowing that the best buzz is always the next day. And we now had that to look forward to as well. Anyone who enjoys a few drinks knows that the next-day pints are unreal. The first half of my work was done, I'd two days off before the Chelsea Bell gig. Happy days.

We got up around nine the next day, jetlagged of course, got the breakfast into us and basically started on the beer. People knew I was in New York, I'd flagged it well in advance, so what would happen was I'd get messages off various people who owned bars inviting us down, laying on free drink and showing us real Irish hospitality. 'Fuck me, Tony,' I said as we hopped from bar to bar, 'this is unreal.'

We ended up meeting Willie Milner, the famous Willie who I had played football with up through the juvenile ranks with Meath and also shared time with in Coláiste Íde.

He had emigrated to America and now we were reunited and on the beer for the day. You'd be just drinking and eating and telling stories and you'd go to pay and they'd say, 'No, that's grand, Rory.' So you'd leave a tip and off you'd go to the next premises. And Tony is like, 'Rory, I need to spend this fucking money! What am I going to do with it?' There was nowhere to spend it unless he went out and bought a suit. And obviously casinos weren't an option because I was done with gambling then.

We had great fun. Stephen Dervan, another childhood friend of mine, worked in a bar there and again we met up with Derv and again we couldn't pay for drink no matter how we tried because he was the barman. We were struggling to spend any money. That night was our last in the hotel for which the Monaghan club had kindly footed the bill. Next day we'd have to check out at noon. And the next night would be my first gig in The Chelsea Bell.

So the following morning, in rag order, we checked out of the hotel. Tony's wife's uncle, Kevin, lives out in the Bronx and was putting us up until the wives arrived. Then we'd stay in a hotel in the city for the remainder. Wouldn't you think we'd considered this a little more? Like the fact I had a gig?

But no, we'd gone out and mad on the beer all day, flat out, in and out of pubs, not thinking of the consequences. So up that morning, dying a death, and we're having to leave this nice hotel. Tony rings Kevin, who tells him there should be a key underneath a flowerpot outside the house. Grand.

Now, I was dying and I had to battle the fear of having to do
a gig that night, and it was one of those stand-up shows. I
was like, *Ah man, how am I going to do this?* But at least we
had a place to stay.

Anyway, we got a taxi out to the house. It was freezing once
we'd left the warmth of the car. There was snow everywhere.
Baltic weather. The taxi dropped us off out in the Bronx,
leaving the two of us lugging these heavy suitcases around.
We had the address and Tony went looking for the key. It
didn't seem to be where he had been told. By now we had
only three hours to spare because I had to be back in the
city to do the gig. Time was moving on and I was starting
to get edgy. 'Tony, where's the key? I've to get changed and I
need a shower!' He rang Kevin, whose phone was off. After
more fruitless searching for the key in the bitter cold, and
with Kevin out of bounds for the time being, it dawned on
us that we were effectively homeless.

I decided to get changed out in the open at the front of
the house, in the sub-zero weather, and started to unpack
my clothes for the gig. And all that time I was cursing Tony,
'You're a fucking eejit, would you not listen to him telling
you where the key's left? It's grand for you, you don't have to
do anything, I've to go and do this fucking show and I don't
even know what I'm going to say on stage!'

We buried the suitcases under the snow in the back
garden. Brought a little carrier bag with whatever bit of
GAA material I had, a football, a ref's jersey, whatever we
could fit in. And we got a train back to the city. Tony said

there was a lovely place for food and drink that he knew of and I badly needed a drink at this stage, so we agreed to head there. I had no stomach for the fear now kicking in from too much drink, which was getting worse the closer it got to the gig. Unlike Sydney, there was no beach nearby that I could run up and down and sweat out the anxiety and certainly no shower available afterwards from which I'd emerge a new man. I needed a beer to settle the nerves. The weather was worsening. We got to this place Tony spoke of, a real American bar, and sat down and ordered two bottles of Bud Light or whatever they were. We ordered food. And I was not in a good place. 'Oh Tony, how am I going to get through this gig tonight, seriously?' And then we were thinking, there's going to be no one at this because of the weather and most Irish people live a bit out of the city.

After the few drinks and a bit of food we pushed on to The Chelsea Bell to face the ordeal. I was in the back of the taxi, Tony seated in the front, but I had my head down looking over the few flimsy preparatory notes that I had for the show. I started to get the spins. I'll never forget, the taxi man pulled up and said, 'Right, that will be 25 dollars.' I said I'd get it but Tony insisted, 'No I'll get it, you've enough on your plate.'

'What do you mean?'

'Look!'

I looked up and saw a restaurant and thought, *this can't be it*. But this was the place. The Chelsea Bell. We walked in anyway and met the owner, who shook my hand, a really nice fella. I asked him where the show was going to take place. 'Oh,' he says, 'that's your stage there.' He pointed to a small platform in the middle of the restaurant where some people were having dinner. Outside of that there was a small group of Irish lads at the bar, like real diehards. They spotted me. 'Ah good boy, Rory's Stories! Ye mad hoor yah!'

I turned to the owner. 'That's the stage? There's no room?'

'No, that's it, that's you there.'

'When do you want me to start?'

'Whenever you're ready.'

'Oh my god.'

It might have been around 8 p.m. We were in a bar/ restaurant. It wasn't a comedy environment. It was like nothing I'd worked in before. People were just having a meal or a drink and here was this absolute lunatic from Ireland about to take over and start talking gibberish. It was mostly Americans in the place. There were only a few there to see me.

The owner was obviously trying to promote the place and I had shared news of the upcoming shows a few times on social media but with the heavy snow and that, people didn't travel in great numbers. There were, I'd say, at a stretch about 12 people there to see me and the others hadn't a bull's notion who I was or what the GAA stood for.

I know there was nobody to blame but myself, but you have to understand that I'm after spending all the day previous on the beer with Tony and I've to change out in the Bronx in the snow. I can feel a chest infection coming on. I needed a hot drink and to get into bed and have someone tell me that everything was going to be OK. Instead I had to put on a show, the fear and dread absolutely crippling me, in front of a small stocious audience that you'd fit into an en suite. I wasn't ready but there was no backing out at this stage.

I got up on stage.

'It's great to be here, anyone ever hear of Rory's Stories?'

Big shout from the corner. 'Gwan ya boy ya!' Mad cunts from Donegal in the corner.

'And what about you over there?'

Silence.

And I looked at Tony and he was pointing at me, laughing, with a bottle of beer in his hand.

I'll never forget the night or the place. Both are branded into my memory till the day I die. I was thinking, *Rory, if you get through this you'll get through anything.* I remember having that thought after around 15 minutes of pain, and knowing I had another half an hour of pain to endure. I texted Tony from the changing room during the interval and he texted back, *I don't care what you are getting paid for this, I wouldn't do it for a million euro.*

I paused with my thoughts for a few moments before going back out to face the audience. *Don't quit. Just get out there and get this done. It is what it is. You shouldn't have gone on the beer yesterday, and it's Tony's fault you got changed in the snow. All is going against you but just do it.*

And I took a deep breath and I walked out on that stage and I had another half an hour of absolute hell.

I slagged Americans. I brought the bouncer up and put a referee's jersey on him and made him do referee stretches. I don't even know what I did. Random stuff to try to pass the time. My confidence was completely on the deck. But I got through it anyway. I had no interest in drinking afterwards. I felt depressed. After the gig I met up with a fella called Enda Williams, an ex-Longford county footballer who was then living in New York. We got a taxi back to the Bronx, which Enda arranged, and Kevin had returned home by then. I had to root my suitcase out of the snow. Into the gaff and lay on the bed. Didn't sleep a wink. It was horrible. The next day the snowfall was so heavy we had to go out with shovels to move the snow, to clear his footpath and drive. But again it comes back to that physical exertion as therapy. Tony said it was the best thing for us. It cleared the heads and sweated out the drink.

Those guys at the bar got a kick out of the show but they were far too drunk to bring on stage. They were just locked. It's bad enough being a singer in the corner of a pub when nobody's listening, but when you're a comedian it's another kettle of fish altogether.

There was this limp clap. The dead-eyed look of the audience. That sinking feeling that this is not going well at all. If your confidence is shot you can't deliver a story, you just want to get through it as quickly as possible and get out of there. Then I had to go back a few days later and do another show there. I was going to give the money back, but, no, I decided to do it. But the second gig was better. It could hardly have been worse.

By this stage the girls had come over to join us. Jen, Tony's wife, came out the day after the first gig and Emma arrived on St Patrick's Day. The second gig was the day after Paddy's Day. I didn't go as mad on the beer the day before this time. And it was a different experience – mercifully, there were more people. It wasn't nearly as bad.

I had way too much craic around New York with Tony for the first show to go well. When it flopped, that was like being punished for being so foolish in the first place. You're young and loose in New York. You're 30 and the beer is free and the hospitality and company is top class. You haven't met Willie Milner in years. The women are going to be over soon. You can make all the excuses. But you will pay the price. It's like that demon resurfacing, pulling you to one side and whispering in your ear, *Right, Rory, you need to experience a bit of downside now, you need to realise that life is not that easy.* That's what is playing over and over in my head. You have to be ready for the ups and downs and that first night in The Chelsea Bell was certainly one of the downs.

Tony was great. He said that in ten years' time nobody will even remember. But it's easy to say that to someone when you're not in their shoes. When you are in those shoes it's you alone, suffering the pain and the shame, and the self-reproach tears you up. Ten years is a long way away when you're lying there on some stranger's bed in the Bronx after a bad gig for which you were largely to blame. It's a bit like telling a footballer after he's lost a county final, 'Ah, you'll be back next year.' True, time is a great healer. But at that precise moment, in the hours after, you can't clear the guilt and misery from your mind.

And the internal conversation is pulling no punches, is apportioning blame. *You didn't prepare properly. You went on the beer.* I can hear my father's voice in my ear as I'm lying on the bed in Kevin's house. *You changed out in the snow. You didn't shower. You didn't sleep. What the fuck did you expect to happen?*

No matter how bad things are, or how low I'm feeling, I still think of The Chelsea Bell when the shit hit the fan and how I got through that. I have a really good mentality on the back of that experience, that no matter what I'm facing I will just get through it. It taught me a really good lesson. As the old saying goes, you learn more from your bad days – that's a fact.

I even knew in The Chelsea Bell that this was going to stand to me. *Just get out there and do it.* I wasn't concerned about people saying the show was terrible – people are going to say that anyway – and I'd a long road ahead to prove myself. But at the time I would have happily handed over ten grand in order to get out of that place and never do comedy again.

Never again will I go on a session the day before a gig. I actually work out the morning of every gig now. And recently, when I was on a tour and had a lot of talks, covering almost 30 events in a month, I went off the beer altogether.

In the early days, when I used to do GAA clubs on a Saturday night, I might get up the next day in great form and have four or five pints just to maintain that buzz I'd had the night before if the gig went well. Then on the Monday I'd feel fairly low because there has to be a comedown. I'd want to get back up there. Now I might go for a run or exercise if I feel the dip. Meet it halfway. You're still going to be a little bit down. That's natural.

People have asked, 'I was at your show last night, there was a standing ovation at the end, what does it feel like?' The only way I can describe it is: your club has won a county final by a point, having not won one for years and you've scored 4–10 from midfield, including the winning score at the end. That's how you feel. I've had some real adrenaline rushes after shows. I used to love nothing more than that feeling of playing a match, knowing you've played well, that deep sense of satisfaction. You're feeling spent and you have a shower, and you come home and you know you left yourself out there on the field. And those bad games where you know you didn't perform, and your hunger wasn't there, that's a real downer. It's no different on the comedy stage, except that you're on your own.

In New York I acted the bollocks to be honest, I didn't make the gigs my priority. But it was part of the process of maturing and growing. For a while I was terrified of the idea of performing in a theatre where you're confined to the stage. When I'm in a GAA club and I tell a story and nobody laughs I have the option of going into the crowd and slagging someone and getting the audience going by another means. You can't do that in a theatre because all you can see is the light shining on you. And I was so afraid of that. *What if they don't laugh?*

I did a gig in a theatre in Dundalk, I began by telling a story and they laughed. I got a massive high that night, felt I'd made a huge leap forward. *I'm in a theatre. I've told stories. I'm not hiding behind a character anymore. I'm not relying on slagging people. I'm telling people stories about my life or my opinion on life and they're laughing and this is where I want to be.*

Next, I went to Sligo. They didn't laugh as much. That's what you learn too. Some don't find it as funny. Audiences and reactions can vary. You need to allow for that and roll with the punches.

I had a fear of Vicar Street because I thought all the best comedians went there and I didn't think I would be able for it. The day I realised I was ready for Vicar Street was the day I did the Dundalk show, when I performed in a full theatre and people laughed at me being me.

I knew then that it was in my own hands. I knew I had the talent in there, but I needed to work at it. No more winging it, Rory. And that's where the exercise came in – looking after myself and putting in the work. There are no short cuts. And I worked hard. The show, *What's the Story, Rory?* that I brought around the country last year, I worked ferociously hard on that. I tried out a lot of material in GAA clubs and eventually I managed to put an hour and 20 minutes of comedy together.

I was in Vicar Street to see Christy Moore the year before I appeared there, and I remember looking around and vowing that I would be there again soon, only this time as the main performance. And I was. And I went to see him there again at Christmas and watched him leave the stage and knew where exactly he was headed backstage. I knew what was behind the curtains, and it was a lovely feeling.

I've been on that stage, I thought to myself, *and I'll be back.*

Chapter 15

Good days and bad days

One summer Sunday in 2018, while with the family on a day out in Howth, Emma pregnant with Zach, I endured one of my worst-ever attacks of depression. Not that you would have known by looking at me, as I didn't let on. I covered it up and pretended all was normal. Kept a brave face. We went down to the pier, the place heaving on a lovely sunny day. Ella was excited by all that was going on around her and I was totally disengaged. I felt numb, distant, like I was running on empty. It's the closest I've been to the kind of emotional state that people must feel when they are near the end. Nothing made me happy. Here we were in Howth, on a gorgeous warm day, I have a 99 in my hand, Emma's happy, strangers are even coming up complimenting me about my work, and I'm in another galaxy. I'm there in body but nowhere near in mind or spirit.

I remember that day vividly and wishing for a long time after that it would never come back again. It has in spurts but not to the same extent. It had been building up gradually over the weekend. It started on the Friday, like a bad weather front slowly approaching. A few showers to begin with, then all of a sudden you're into a full-scale storm. If you were in Howth that day and recognised me you might have thought: there's Rory O'Connor – he's everything going for him, he took a chance and now he's living the dream. And you'd have no idea of the turmoil going on inside my head. If a stranger had come up to me that day and hit me a box on the mouth I probably wouldn't have hit him back. I was gone. I had no fight left.

Because I'd opened up about mental health and written about it extensively, I felt a duty not to surrender easily or allow myself break down. Weak as it left me, I would have to wade through this. But that did not make this depression any easier to manage or endure. I dearly wanted to not feel like this. When it passes on, as it always does, and you feel good again you wonder why you felt like that in the first place. You try to pinpoint possible underlying reasons. But sometimes there are no obvious explanations. It can strike without warning, leaving you unprepared.

Emma and I get on so well, we've known each other a long time and we're easy in each other's company. But there's times I can't look her in the eye. I feel ashamed. I'm too weak internally. I might say it to her when the depression passes but at the time I'm struck dumb and I suffer in silence.

There is a local charity in Ashbourne called ASAP (Ashbourne Suicide Awareness and Prevention), which locals formed after several suicides occurred in the area.

Eugene Kennedy was one of the main people behind its
formation. One of their mottos is 'Talk on your good days'
and to me that is brilliant advice. When you're not feeling
OK, it's so incredibly difficult to talk. I know that myself.
That day in Howth, I just couldn't say it to Emma. It's like
being in a prison cell and only you can see the bars, they are
invisible to everyone else around you.

So when you're better, talk about it. When you're in
the throes of despair, you can't tie your shoelaces. Your
confidence is on the floor. And when you're a public figure
as I am to some extent, when you're recognised and stared
at, it's horrible if you happen to be suffering from one of
those episodes. When I'm feeling like that, I avoid public
places. There's days when I'm just not able for it, I'm too
anxious.

My way of battling depression is through exercise. By
moving my body every day, I keep it at bay. It's a formula
that works for me. Paul Clarke, who managed us for a couple
of years, was also keen on personal fitness. At one stage he
had to undergo a groin operation that ruled out exercise
for a while. We were in the clubhouse bar after training one
Sunday morning. Clarkey would be a fairly upbeat man but
that day he was very quiet. I went up to him and asked,
'How's the body?'

'It's not great, have to be honest with you – only for youse
keeping me going I don't know where my head would be at.'

And I thought, *Jeez that was fairly deep*. But it was only
afterwards I realised that Clarkey was on the money there.

And I'm very like him. He was used to doing all these runs, he had a regular routine. But after he got his operation, he didn't have his outlet. So he channelled his energy into the club and that kept him going.

I hope people reading this book can learn something from it. I wish I'd had something like that to cling to when I was 15. I might have been able to say to myself, *Well, if he can do it, then maybe there's something in it for me.*

While I was never diagnosed with any personality disorder, I definitely feel I have a touch of something. When I get excited I start rubbing my hands really quickly. Sometimes I could start yelping in the middle of the kitchen, for example, for no apparent reason. That is some disorder, I don't know what it is. My dad has it as well. You can swing from one extreme mood to another and you just have to know that the difficult periods will pass.

Calling a halt to gambling obviously reduced the number of times I'd beat myself up, but the urge is still there. It'll always be there. When I hit a chronic low, I'd always talk to someone. I think of the likes of Robin Williams and others, how they couldn't take it anymore. And I have that madness. I try to embrace it, use it positively, but it's not always that straightforward. I'm only 33 now and I'm up and down. Hard physical exertion as a means of banishing negative energy didn't start on Coogee Beach. I was only 12 or 13 when I got a bench press for Christmas and I got a bike the following year. I was always into fitness and activity – and even at that stage it was becoming a means of healing, although I wouldn't have known it myself. It wasn't a conscious decision at the time, like later in life, but the same motives were at play. I was cementing the relationship between vigorous exercise and a positive mental outlook.

I had a boxing bag in the garden shed. My dad made one up for me. He got an old coal sack and filled it with sand and tied it to a rope and I mean if you caught this bag wrong it'd break your wrist. I'd beat the shit out of it for half an hour at a time. That bag took the brunt of a lot of teenage frustration. Another thing I would do was swing it and hit it a shoulder as it came back and it fucking hurt. And I'd do it again and again, and I'd come back out of the shed in better form. It was often cold in there and I'd put on a pair of football gloves and go for it, emptying myself of whatever was within that needed to be emptied.

I can be unduly hard on myself, like a lot of people are, but the key is not to bottle it up, whether that means talking to someone or beating the daylights out of a bag in your garden shed. I'd get lifts to work on days after losing football matches and be physically sick with disappointment. I don't know why I put so much pressure on myself – maybe because Gaelic football was the only thing I knew I was half-decent at. I didn't give a shit about school. I didn't care if I got a bad report, but if I played poorly in a game, it would have a serious impact on my form.

It's that thing of having a certain personality that appears outgoing and upbeat, the life and soul of the party, and later finding that someone fitting this description is severely depressed. You have to take every day as it comes. I can't say that when I'm 60 those thoughts won't be less severe. I don't know.

But I do know there's help there and I know I'll ask for it when the depression gets severe. And if I need medication, I'll take it. If I need to give up alcohol for ever, I'll do it. Anything to make sure I'm here tomorrow. That's what I have learned over the years, that your mental health will be your hardest battle.

So what would I do if I can't exercise like I normally do? I've taken up golf again, which I've found is one of the best outlets. You leave the phone in the bag and get on that tee box and for the guts of four hours you're just playing golf. There's no social media, no Rory's Stories, no distractions. I play with a lot of my friends who couldn't be arsed about Rory's Stories and that's perfect. It's a sense of being normal, I suppose. And you might play badly but it doesn't really matter. You're out there, getting fresh air, chatting to people. You're miles away from your daily life.

In 2015 the Cycle Against Suicide came to Ashbourne. Over 800 people die by suicide each year in Ireland and the indications are that thousands more contemplate it. I opened up about my story, about how I asked for help, and related the time I started Rory's Stories and found a positive space for my energy. The Society organised a 50k-cycle around Meath and I got roped in. I used a banger of a bike and the hole was killing me for a week after. I wasn't used to cycling. My legs were fine but my arse was in bits, me in a pair of Donaghmore-Ashbourne shorts, and everyone else in their proper gear.

Jim Breen, the founder of Cycle Against Suicide, asked me to say a few words afterwards. I found it a bit daunting. Even though I was well used to speaking before an audience, this was a different setting. I wasn't there to make anyone laugh. Also, it was the first time I opened up publicly about my gambling. I was revealing that I had been in a dark place, that I went for help. I spoke of the mental health issues I'd encountered. All that was new territory and exposure. Making it even tougher was the fact that there were a lot of people present that I knew a long time and I was telling them my story. It was a local audience. I wasn't anonymous but well known. Jim gave me a hug when it was over and explained that these personal revelations and lessons were invaluable. I felt great after it.

Opening up is not a natural Irish trait. My mam would be like, 'Oh, don't be talking too much about the gambling, you don't want people to be thinking ...' Typical Irish mother, worrying about what other people think. I listen to my mam and dad but I am very much my own person now. I tried to explain, *Mam, I need to open up here for people to look at me and say, well look at what Rory has done.* My goal was to try to help others not trip up the same way as I had done. If that came with some embarrassing personal details being revealed, so what? It was a small price to pay and it meant that at least I was able to take something useful from those difficult years.

So I did that for Jim, I opened up and told everything. Then I was asked to go on another Suicide Awareness cycle around Cork where I met up with Conor Cusack, the former Cork hurler, who has been exceptionally frank about his mental health issues. I had some of the best days of my life on this excursion. We cycled from Cork city all the way to Bantry and around west Cork. We stayed in random people's houses, people who had been directly affected by suicide and who were willing to put the cyclists up. They'd cook you dinner at night. But it was the conversations around dinner that gave you a deeper insight into the impact suicide has on lives, where maybe a family would be talking about their young son and the lead-up to when he took his life. I was completely absorbed. It put me thinking of my cousin and my own spells feeling particularly low. Hearing these other tragic stories deepened my conviction that I could contribute something positive in helping to tackle this plague. I felt a kind of calling. I needed to drive this message home.

I went on to speak in maybe four or five different primary and secondary schools over those days. I'd spend maybe ten minutes telling my story, and then put out a few messages like the importance of asking for help as I had done myself. Some of the students had seen the videos and when they recognise you they tend to listen more attentively. That helps when you're talking to a young audience, whose attention can sometimes wander.

In 2019 the Construction Industry Federation (CIF) asked me as work as an ambassador on their behalf, which involved going round to different sites and talking to the workers about mental health. So I was going in and speaking to groups of anything from 30 to 400 people. Depending on numbers they'd be in the canteen or out in a large open-air location. I took a personal pride and interest in these talks because I knew I was the perfect fit. I was not unlike many of the lads I was talking to and I'd done a lot of building-site sketches so I was also relatively well known. Lads listened to me. And I was coming in with no educated lingo or anything, I was saying, 'Lads, this is the fucking craic. Here's what happened me. I was shit in school. I asked for help and now I'm doing this.' I felt elated after those talks, and at least one person would come up to me and say, 'Rory, here's my story.' One man showed me his wrists that he'd slit ten years before, and thankfully he was in a better place now. Another fella came up and asked me about exercise and told me how much he related to my story about exercise being a foil against depression. It was amazing.

Other talks followed, organisations seeing a value in someone that their employees might listen to because I was just an ordinary fella with a problem who needed help and support and lived to tell the tale. The central message was that if you are feeling like this, you are not alone and there is nothing to be ashamed of. You just need to reach out for help.

Since 2015, when Rory's Stories became more widely known, I've often shared social media posts about mental health. And I still do. I've made a small number of videos that created different scenarios around mental health. These videos, combined, have had around four million views. But it's not about the number of views; it's about the hope that one person, having watched one of those videos, might think about reaching out for help. Paddy, Tony and Owen Andrews ('Snako') came in to assist me and play the characters. One was for the Cycle Against Suicide. Another I came up with myself: you see a group of fellas enjoying a party, then one of them is leaning over a bridge and being spoken to by his friends who persuade him not to jump into the water. I wanted to nail that person who was the life and soul of the party but who was hiding serious depression from the world. We shot another video of a lad in the GAA changing room telling jokes. Then you see him, the same evening, contemplating suicide. Those videos attracted a lot of views and commentary.

I did another last year of two lads having an open conversation in a car where they share their most private thoughts and feelings. We made it look so normal to have this talk, encouraging people to be open. That got a massive response online as well.

What speaks volumes to me about the importance of mental health in the country is that no matter where I go outside of Ashbourne, be it to a pub, restaurant or wherever, I hear the same thing. 'Howya, Rory, I think you're a gas man but I love your mental health work. Thank you.' Then the person will walk away, message delivered. Or it could be in a bar and a lad comes up and says he just wants to shake your hand, and you know why and he'll squeeze your hand and walk away. This happens so much. For some, these videos and messages offer a way of expressing how they feel. They make it alright to feel like this. Often they don't have to say very much at all for you to understand that something you've done has helped in some way. Yet nobody in Ashbourne comes up to me. Why? Because they know me as Rory O'Connor and they don't want Rory to think they're depressed. That's the stigma. That's where the problem is. People are afraid of what others think of them.

For the CIF alone I might have spoken to over 10,000 people. For Health and Safety Week last year I was doing a minimum of two talks a day, in different parts of the country but mainly around Dublin. In the last couple of years I've really ramped up on mental health and used my profile to sell the message because I know how much it is helping. I put up a post a while back about me going through the 'black dog' for a few days. Just to show I'm normal. When the black dog left me I was upset with myself for a while that I'd put it up there. I started asking myself questions. *Why did you do it? Are you looking for sympathy?*

And when I calmed down I realised it had nothing to do with ego or self-promotion, but more a conviction that this might help someone else. I have some influence, and those people suffering with their mental health might just listen to me. I want to be honest with my followers and let them know what I go through from time to time. *Hey, I felt shit for the last couple of days.* Because feeling shit happens to everyone. No one should feel they're alone in this.

I still do a lot of schools because that is an area close to my heart. Even more so when I am asked to talk to those on Youthreach, the school leavers' programme. Youthreach provides two years of integrated education, training and work experience for unemployed early school leavers without any qualifications or vocational training who are between 15 and 20 years of age. I like going to Youthreach talks because I believe that a lot of those who end up there are misunderstood. They are boys and girls who in some cases have been kicked out of school. Some may have already given up on life – I can tell by their body language. I believe a lot of them just need an arm over the shoulder and to be told that they have potential.

That's why I enjoy going into those meetings saying that all I have in my arse pocket is an LCA certificate. That's it. Yet I'm a bestselling author. I've sold shows all over the country. I've been on RTÉ. I'm no smarter than you. I just fucking asked for help. Found out what I was good at and worked my bollocks off, worked really hard every day to achieve that. I tell them they can do whatever they want to do. Don't let school define you, or teachers who said you'd amount to nothing. Your whole life is ahead of you. I didn't turn the corner until I was in my mid-20s. If even one of them paid heed and it helped change their outlook and made a difference, it'll have been worth it.

I did around a dozen talks for the ESB recently as well. My feeling is that I'm beginning to change people's thoughts on mental health and starting to break this thing down. Now a lot of people are doing great work, the likes of Bressie and others.

I had to hit the bottom to force myself to say I needed help. I know how difficult it is to say those few words. Nobody wants to die by suicide. People would rather do it than open up, which is a terrible state of affairs. So the more people who open up the more it makes it easier for others. I feel so sorry for the older generation in Ireland. So many suffered desperately with mental health issues and had no help or acknowledgement. What strong people they were.

Money and all the trappings of fame mean nothing. Denzel Washington says the most valuable currency is helping others, and I firmly believe that. I get enormous satisfaction out of helping people in any way I can. Money can't buy that.

It can be a tough battle minding your mental health with all life throws at you, but when you have a public profile and one that has benefited from social media to get your name known, there is an inevitable downside. You become what some people see as a legitimate target. There are people you have never met, nor ever will, who see that target and who can't let the chance pass to take aim. You might not be ready for that until it happens.

Chapter 16

Social media

The videos I've been shooting with Enya Martin usually play on the nature of close relationships and try to convey everyday situations in a comic light. Two people living under the one roof over an extended period of time, no matter how compatible, are bound to have moments when the sparks flying aren't always those of a romantic kind. Many of these videos struck a chord with people. At times there may have been a useful message included, some food for thought, but they were mainly designed to get a laugh and to make people feel better. We exaggerate situations for comic effect – find some human aspect or pattern of behaviour and blow it up.

In August 2018 we had this idea of a comedy sketch where a man gets home from work tired and just wants to relax. He's worn out after a long day and barely in the door when his partner suddenly hits him with a flurry of questions. He gets a hundred questions at once. 'How was your day?' 'Did you put out the bins?' 'What are you doing tonight?' 'Did you go to the post office?' All this kind of stuff.

And he's like, 'Just give me a minute to relax!'

Enya and I discussed the idea and we were on the same wavelength. She felt it was worth doing, it had potential and the ring of truth but fun as well. She came over and we filmed it more or less off the cuff. My mother, who is as inoffensive as they come and who would have a censor's eye, did the filming, and we all got a great laugh out of it. My dad watched it too, and found it funny, and it went up online that night.

The next day Emma, Ella and I were heading to Lahinch for a break. It is a part of the world we like to escape to from time to time. Before we left I checked how the video was doing and it seemed to be getting a lot of hits. Thought nothing more of it. Then we hit the road. In August Lahinch is busy with holidaymakers, people drawn in large numbers to the beach or the famous links golf course. From there you can quickly reach a number of scenic spots in west Clare.

We arrived, checked in to one of the local hotels, and felt immediately at ease, determined to completely switch off and enjoy the time together. I had a second book in the pipeline, enough to keep me busy. Life was good. The next day the plan was to drive up the road a few miles past Liscannor and visit the Cliffs of Moher. Sometimes I like leaving my phone behind and being completely out of bounds and free. This was one such occasion. I deliberately left it in the hotel room.

We drove on to Doolin from where we took a boat to the base of the Cliffs of Moher just below O'Brien's Tower.

And as luck would have it, two lads who happened to be followers of Rory's Stories were in charge of the boat. They brought me and Ella up front and got Ella to hold the captain's steering wheel and we got a great view of the cliffs. It was just a lovely day spent having quality time with the family.

By the time we got back to the hotel it was maybe five o'clock and I hadn't looked at my phone since around nine that morning. The first thing I noticed was a missed call from Enya. Then a missed call from Al Foran, the impressionist, who I've become very friendly with in recent years. A missed call from Dave, my manager. And a text from Paddy, who had sent a message saying something like, *Ah don't mind it, Rory.*

Puzzled, I texted Enya to see if there was anything up. She replied: *Have you checked Twitter?*

I went on and I will never forget it. There were numerous notifications on my Twitter app, which has happened plenty of times in the past, especially when I've been tweeting during a match or releasing new videos. But I couldn't think of any reason for this heightened activity now. I pressed the button.

You're are a disgrace.

You are the most unfunny thing ever.

I rang Enya. She was a bit upset. 'Oh Rory, my Twitter's exploding, I'm getting messages online about domestic violence, I had a newspaper want to know if you forced me to make this video!'

I rang Dave. He was really calm. 'Listen Rory, you ruffled a few feathers, it'll blow over. Forget about it.'

Literally every five minutes I was getting fresh notifications on Twitter. 'Emma,' I'd go, 'look at this!' All that peace and tranquillity, that sense of being disconnected from work and the day job, was now shattered. The content was serious and couldn't be easily ignored. One tweet claimed that Rory's Stories was an advertisement for domestic violence, and that when I banged the table it reminded him of his father hitting his mother. It's something that never even crossed my mind. Domestic violence is a terrible thing, and the last thing I want to do is upset people – I want my sketches to be funny. We'd created a shitstorm. I didn't know what to do.

In the video I play the flustered husband arriving home from work and when the wife asks one question too many, barely giving him time to answer the ones she's asked already, he loses his patience. He feels like he is facing an inquisition. He accuses her of being 'up me hole' the minute he arrives in the door. The language is raw in places – I throw a few 'fucks' across the table – but the impression we were trying to give was of a man at his wits' end and his wife at her wits' end. And Enya did a brilliant job of the wife giving him a grilling.

I had not thought the video could be interpreted in such a way, and the comments I was receiving were vitriolic. Of course domestic violence is not something that should be made light of, and it was never my intention to offend anyone, but anyone who is active on social media, no matter how many followers you have, knows that it's not a place where you can talk things through. Reactions are instant, off the cuff.

Emma told me to forget about it. We were away, it was not the time. So I put my phone down, and we went out for dinner and there was a man and a woman at the bar, and I looked up and the man says, 'Ah, Rory's Stories, good man, fair play to you, myself and herself were watching that video you did last night, that's us all the time, she'd be in my ear, and you're a gas fella.'

Here was a random stranger saying this to my face, telling me how much this same video had made him and his wife laugh, with no hint of him being offended or seeing anything objectionable in the content. Not that this, though appreciated, was what I was paying most attention to. I was being driven to distraction by negative comments rather than those that were positive. This was a lesson I had to learn, which came with being in the spotlight. I needed to realise it's possible for my content to be interpreted differently than I intended, and that while I certainly meant no offence, some people found it upsetting. I have to live with that and just know that my intentions were good and that in no way would I ever want to promote domestic violence, no matter what people were implying. I could not allow those comments get inside my head or hijack my emotions. Emma could see that I wasn't myself. I told her I was trying to put it to one side, and not let it ruin our time away. I was looking at Ella, who was only five at the time, and I was trying to be happy for her sake. I had a couple of messages from newspapers looking for a quote from me, but I said nothing.

What sickened me was people who have always hated Rory's Stories coming out of the woodwork. They all started jumping on this. It reminded me of being in a schoolyard and having everyone weighing in, bullies coming from everywhere, kicking you while you were down. People who never liked my comedy and were jealous of my success came from everywhere and were jumping on the bandwagon, having a go. It had suddenly become a free-for-all. It wasn't about the video anymore – it was just a pile-on.

I told you about Rory's Stories from the get-go.

It was tempting to go on the defensive, as I was upset and felt people were painting me in a light that didn't reflect my intentions or who I am, but I had to hold back. I had no interest in any pints or anything else, so we went back to the hotel room. Even though I told myself not to look at my phone again, before I knew it I'd be checking for fresh notifications. I was trying to be calm, but the truth was that I was distraught.

Eventually Emma fell asleep and I put the phone down and I lay there allowing the thing to work through my mind, allowing the impulse to write back to pass, not to do something rash that I'd regret later. When my mind is addled like that it is not conducive to a good night's sleep. I think it must have been about five in the morning when, after a fitful sleep, on and off, I heard Ella getting up to go to the toilet. I was wide awake. I got out of bed quietly and just felt that I needed to get some air, so I put on a pair of runners and while I was doing this Emma woke. 'Where are you going?' she asked.

'Ah, I'm just going out to clear my head.'

She hesitated. I knew she was thinking that I'd go off and do something stupid.

'Emma, honestly, I'm fine, I just need to go and clear my head.'

'Are you sure?'

'Yes, I'm fine. I'll go for a run.'

It was actually lashing rain that morning in Lahinch, but I didn't care. I had to take my frustration out some way and staying cooped up in a hotel bedroom, unable to sleep properly, wasn't going to cut it. So I decided I'd run it out. The beach was virtually empty at that hour, which was perfect. I sprinted up and down Lahinch beach in the pissing rain and now and then I found myself shouting at the sky.

'Come on! I'm ready for you! You won't get the better of me!'

And if you'd seen a grown man behaving like this, running madly in the rain at this early hour while most of the world was still asleep, yelling like some demented lunatic at the heavens, you might have been tempted to call for the men in white coats. Lonely as the beach was at that hour, I noticed there was a woman out walking and I'd say she was saying someone should put that lad in a straitjacket. I was punching fresh air. I was so upset.

I didn't think I had done anything wrong. This was just my take on the stupid fights you have with your partner. Whatever about my mental well-being, those leaving negative comments were doing a fantastic job improving my physical fitness levels. I must have run up and down the beach for 45 minutes. I think I actually hurt my hamstring at one stage I was sprinting that quickly. My body was numb, it was cold at that hour, it was wet but I didn't care. I ran and I ran. It reminded me of that time in Australia when I was fighting the demons. But these were different demons; these weren't alcohol-related, they were pressure-related. I ran and I ran and I ran and then I came back, I had a shower and I felt a lot better. It worked. I'm not going to say that I completely forgot about what was agitating me, but it did me the world of good, and about two days later the furore died down.

Social media is a double-edged sword. It opened up doors for me in so many ways, but the pressures of it will find you anywhere, even on a quiet family holiday in Lahinch, and you need to do your best to not let it take over.

I was due to bring out my book in the few weeks that followed and I had lined up a good bit of advance PR to promote it but a lot of those plans fell through because of this controversy. But I decided in this case it was better to not add fuel to the fire, so I didn't respond online.

From that video experience I realised that no matter what I do, even if I were to cure cancer, I was always going to have these haters and knockers. Others were, I felt, misguided, even if they had no previous axe to grind with me. Anonymous keyboard warriors were claiming that this was promoting domestic abuse or normalising violence in the home. It was the worst spell of online vitriol I've had to deal with. I'd got it previously in dribs and drabs but never this barrage. I ultimately felt that there were people out there who supported me and found it funny, and that was why I kept the video up.

Kevin Hart, the American stand-up comedian, has spoken about the benefits of fitness training in times of acute stress. He works out every day but when he was going through a period of turmoil with his wife after an infidelity episode, which attracted a lot of publicity, he upped his workouts to three times a day to keep himself mentally stable. I'm not condoning Hart's infidelity, but what he said about the benefits of exercise in fighting off depression rang a bell with me.

It was also lovely, through all that difficult time, to get supportive messages on social media. And those people I met in Lahinch who were complimentary were also a great help in raising my spirits and reminding me that I had to hold firm for their sakes too and repay their loyalty by moving on from what had happened and continuing to try to make people laugh.

I mainly use Twitter now to promote mental health. And being candid about mental health on social media and through giving talks can help people. At a match in Croke Park last year with Emma, a fella called me out of the crowd, a man in a Kerry jersey, I'd say in his 50s. He came over and he gave me the strongest hug I've ever had. I noticed he had tears in his eyes. Then he said, 'I had to meet you, you've saved my life. You've done so much for me.'

And I said to Emma, 'You know what? I actually don't care if nobody finds me funny anymore.'

What I've done to help people like him is more important than comedy, and that to me is up there with any high on the stage, any successful gig I ever did.

Sometimes I delete my social media for a couple of days. There are times when its waters are not a safe place to swim if you're feeling vulnerable. If you dip in and see something that needles you, it can be hard to wriggle off the hook. It might end up preoccupying you for the whole day. You find yourself paying too much attention to negative comments. You let them creep under your skin. You read too much negativity and take too much to heart. This is the darker side of social media. There's no doubting that it has been a useful resource for information about mental health and yet it can also be the cause of depression and stress. I find it useful to turn it off for a couple of days every now and then just to get a breather.

We live in a faster world than we did years ago. And it's only getting faster. There's a lot more pressure on everyone in a world reflected through social media. There are benefits – having a large following gives me a platform to raise awareness around mental health – but social media is not a substitute for real life.

Freedom of speech online is important, but it should come with responsibility, for both those who create online content and those who comment on it. I've learned that I have a responsibility as a content creator, but those responsible for hurtful personal attacks need to understand the impact they are having. You see these users hiding behind an egg on their profile picture and abusing people all day – that is not on. I talked to Pat Spillane on the topic recently and he said he would have received hate mail from opposition supporters in his letterbox – he said it got to the stage where he just wouldn't look at them, the postman would bin them. But when it's on your phone it's open season, a free-for-all; it is not as easily ignored. All you can do is switch it off or delete your account. I would recommend to anyone who feels that social media is making them feel worse than better to just delete their account.

When I started putting up Rory's Stories videos some of the stuff you'd read in the comments section was beyond disgusting, sickening personal threats to members of my family. I talk about believing in yourself and doing something you enjoy yet it's difficult to do that because of the age we live in, because of the people who delight in bringing you down. No matter what you put up online, some people won't like it. That's what Paddy Houlihan from *Mrs Brown's Boys* told me, and he was right. I came from rock-bottom, so I have thick skin. But I can see why people give up on their dreams because of what others think. And that's why I want to use my career to change people's mindsets, let young people be free and be what they want to be without the negativity. Cyberbullying has to stop.

The government needs to address this and have a programme of education in the schools in response to the rise in online bullying and abuse. A report in the UK last year showed one in four social media users claimed to have suffered some form of cyberbullying. Some people just get a kick out of trolling and upsetting people. Parents have to be on top of what's going on in their children's social media. I hope that these trolls and vultures find a better human understanding and row back, and that they realise they need to stop this because it is damaging lives, and in some tragic cases it is ending them.

Chapter 17

Vicar Street

A few years ago the publishers Gill suggested that I write a book. I'd enjoyed writing those blogs at the early stages of Rory's Stories, but this was like asking me to swim in a lake filled with crocodiles. I thought, *can I do this?* But terrifying as it was, I decided I wanted to. I wanted to prove that I could, despite all my fears and feelings of inadequacy that went back to the classroom.

And then, of course, I got the bit between my teeth. I remember ringing Gill constantly, probably wrecking their heads, but I looked on the book's completion a bit like that wall I took the Kango to in Australia. One side of me was advising caution: *You can't spell. You were in LCA.* The other was saying, *Fuck it, prove them all wrong.*

Everyone laughed when I told them I was writing a book. But it became my obsession. I used to get up at 4.30 a.m. and go for a little jog and come back and start writing at 5 a.m. for two hours, three days a week. I googled and researched about authors and poets, when they are at their sharpest, and discovered that the best time seemed to be very late at night or very early in the mornings. So I followed that advice. And mornings worked for me.

I put my head down, let the stories flow, didn't mind the spelling, and before I knew it the book was done. I still can't believe I did it. It was a bestseller and if anything, Gill probably underestimated its potential. After that success they asked could I do another. I thought about it for a while. I thought that plenty might have said, 'Ah sure, anyone can write a book on the GAA. But can he do a second one?' So the following year I went at it hammer and tongs and wrote another one. It stressed the bollocks out of me but I got it done and it was another bestseller. I wanted to prove I could do it again. And I did.

And I can't help thinking back to St Declan's when I was out in the hall, all those years wandering aimlessly, and here I was now: Rory O'Connor, bestselling author. I bring those two books to all my talks because I think it's a powerful example of how I didn't allow my limitations defeat me. I couldn't spell, I was often kicked out of class and I didn't have a Leaving Cert, but I could still produce two successful books. It is probably what I am most proud of because to do that was a big psychological challenge for me. I had to push the boundaries to make that happen and I don't mind admitting that I am proud of those feats considering where I'd started.

Another example of pure doggedness getting results was around 2016 when I decided I should try to get Rory's Stories on television. At the time *Republic of Telly* was a popular comedy show. To say I hounded RTÉ is an understatement. I must have sent 30–40 emails a week for months, inviting them to look at my work. The odd time you'd get an email back to say, *Thanks for getting in touch. We will be back if we need anything.*

I'd kind of given up on it. Then one day I was sitting at home and I got this message on Facebook from a fella called Shane Mulvey, a producer on the show, asking if I would be interested in meeting for a chat. I thought this was a prank, one of the lads acting the bollocks on me. So I messaged back, said it sounded great, and asked for an email. That showed that it was legit.

I met with him and a co-writer in Donnybrook. He said they had been following me for a while and that there was an opening to do a bit of work with them. They had me in a few sketches which they scripted that I didn't think were that funny, it wasn't my kind of humour really. They did this thing where I dressed up as Paul O'Connell, the Irish rugby player. Now it was grand, but I didn't think it was that funny myself. I think I could have done a better job.

Then the dream moment happened when they said that they'd like me to do a sketch based on the characters in a GAA club. I said, 'Now you're fucking talking. This is my area.' We shot it here in the local club in Ashbourne. I remember being here two years earlier with Paddy making the sketches on my iPhone 4 and now I was back with the RTÉ cameras. And I thought this was an amazing transformation, a sign that things were really happening for me.

Paddy was also involved in the sketches and we would go into the studio on a Sunday night when the show was recorded. They asked if I would do a bit of comedy to get the audience warmed up before the show. This is where I was out of my comfort zone – not many of these people, I suspected, knew who I was or my line of comedy.

I didn't have any kind of script. I had to keep it relevant, it had to be a GAA theme. So the idea I came up with was that we were playing *The Late Late Show* in the county final at the weekend and we needed a key man to mark Ryan Tubridy. So I walk around the audience, bring some of them down and rip the piss for ten minutes. I think it went well. They asked me back a couple of times to do the warm-up routine.

At one point I was sitting at the side of the stage, where all these famous RTÉ shows are filmed, seeing the audience and then my face on the screen. A year ago I'd been hassling RTÉ to give me a chance; now here I was, looking at myself on the screen, and it was a lovely feeling, I won't lie, I had a great sense of fulfilment. Now I hadn't reached the holy grail but this was a huge step forward.

Even in the green room after, drinking and having the craic, it was such a savage feeling. Then being on the telly that following Monday night and being at home in Ashbourne and seeing the head on me there and, even more important, seeing the club displayed and me wearing the club tracksuit. That filled me with pride.

I think I did around three sketches in total, one around a county final and another based on pre-season. Going on the

YouTube stats, they were very successful. They had around half a million views. Then *Republic of Telly* went belly up. But it gave me a hope that if you keep trying you will get there. It was a lesson in persistence.

Then Aiken Promotions invited me to do a tour and asked if I wanted Vicar Street included. Initially I said no. I felt I wasn't ready for it yet. They said that we would do Liberty Hall instead, a smaller 450-seater. When Dave sent me the poster, my nerves were shot. *Who's going to come and see me?* I thought. Little by little venues started selling out, then Liberty Hall sold out before Christmas and it wasn't scheduled until the following March. Liberty Hall went very well but to be honest the minute I stepped off stage in Dundalk (the first show on the tour) I knew I was ready do Vicar Street. Once I had done that first show I was confident that I could do the rest.

Over 900 people turned up to see me in Vicar Street. Dave came in during the interval saying that Shane Lowry wanted to say hello. Shane, his brother Alan, Conor Moore from *Conor's Sketches*, the Kilkenny hurler Richie Hogan, the actor Lar Kinlan from *Love/Hate* and the successful pub-owner Alan Clancy, to name a few, were all drinking in the backstage bar. Conor and I would be fairly close, we've known each other a few years and we've helped each other out. I'm extremely proud of him doing so well, and having made such a big impact, not just here but abroad. All the lads were fairly well oiled because they were at the All-Ireland final the same day, and they were just having banter, but my head was spinning. I was focused completely on the show, reflecting on how the first half had gone, thinking about the next half. It was like playing a match except you're on your own up there.

I'd met Shane Lowry before then in slightly unusual circumstances. Around Christmas 2018, having had a good year, I'd booked Emma and me into the Shelbourne Hotel for a night. We were going to see Christy Moore in Vicar Street. Emma was getting ready and I put up a photo of myself on Instagram lying on the bed in the Shelbourne. I got a message from Shane ten minutes later saying, *Well horse, are you out for the night? I'm over in O'Donoghue's if you fancy a drink?* So I says to Emma, 'Ah jaysus, we can't turn down a drink with Lowry.' So we skipped dinner, which she wasn't too happy about.

Shane was there with his coach, Neil Manchip, and we were drinking away, having the craic. And I said, 'Do you fancy coming to Christy Moore with us?' They hadn't any tickets. So Shane made a few calls and nothing came up. So I said, 'Come on, you'll be grand.' Anyway, we went down, the four of us, and Lowry ended up getting two tickets off a tout. We got in and had an unreal night.

Afterwards I got a text saying they were in the Oak Bar near Vicar Street, which is owned by Alan Clancy, who Shane introduced me to. Alan asked if we fancied going back to another one of his bars, House, where they were hosting a party for Hozier. We got into his jeep and headed down to Leeson Street and straight in the front door to the VIP area.

Lo and behold, there was Hozier, a big hoor, probably an inch or two taller than me. Built like a matchstick. Big long Edward Scissorhands head on him.

I went up and introduced myself. Said I'd made a few videos. He said he had seen some and liked them, and he couldn't have been a nicer fella. And there were a couple of lads present from the band Kodaline. So I had an unbelievable night. Talking mostly to Shane Lowry about football. He is more interested in talking about football than about golf. We were chatting about Matt Connor and famous Meath footballers and all of that. We drank into the night and that was the end of it.

After that I texted Alan Clancy to thank him for his hospitality and ask if he might be interested in lunch because I felt he would be a man worth talking to. So we met in Avoca in Clonee. I wanted to pick his brain about business and opportunities and he was very sound. He really was. Shane Lowry had won a tournament in Abu Dhabi around January 2019 and Alan said they were having a few drinks in House to celebrate the win a couple of weeks later. He said that if I was interested in coming, there would be a few people present that might be work talking to.

So myself and Emma went into town and had a few drinks and then headed up to House and announced we were there for the Shane Lowry party. The guy on the door said there wasn't one. *Oh my god*, I thought, *I'm after being pranked at the highest level possible.* I rang Alan Clancy, who didn't answer. Then Alan rang back. We were at the wrong venue. The party was being held at 37 Dawson Street. By now I was getting a bit nervous, felt we might be out of our comfort zone here. And then we were halfway up the stairs when I heard, 'Ah, you big Offaly bollocks ya!' Offaly accents. *Ah we'll be at home here*, I figured. We walked on in. Alan introduced me to a few people. I spotted Robbie Keane and his wife. A.P. McCoy was there as well. Danny from The Coronas. Mary Black. I decided to approach Robbie Keane.

'Hi, Robbie, my name is Rory.'

'Ah hi Rory, I've seen some of your stuff online.'

I introduced Emma. He goes, 'Hi Emma, my name is Robbie.'

I was going, 'Robbie she knows who you are.'

He goes, 'It's still nice to introduce yourself, Rory.'

And I thought, *that was pure class*. He was there with his wife Claudine who was really friendly and considerate in making sure Emma didn't feel left out.

As the night went on I was saying to Robbie that I found him very humble for a guy who was an Irish sporting legend. And he said, 'I'm from Tallaght – why would I go around thinking I'm better than anyone else? I'm just good at football. You have to remain thankful and humble.' And that stuck with me. It was a great night mingling with all the stars but what Robbie Keane said to me stood out. It was the same with Christy Dignam when I met him. He also has that humility.

But it's still a bit surreal being in the company of people with that kind of profile. I suppose it's something that takes getting used to. I was at the golf pro-am in Lahinch last year with Cormac McGill and my dad. Cormac is high up in the guards and keeps me on the straight and narrow, he's always been a good friend. Paul O'Connell walked up to a tee box. I was looking at Paul, a bit in awe. Next thing he goes, 'Ah, good man Rory, I'm a huge fan.' I froze on the spot. *My god, did he just say that?* I couldn't wait to go over and tell my oul lad, who was looking the other way. That was one of those moments where you felt ten feet tall. And a little bit later he came up, offered his hand and we had a few words. I turned to the boys and said, 'Lads, I'm going on the beer now, that's as happy as I can be.' And I ended up having a great night in Lahinch. But it's very revealing how people like that behave off camera. The success hasn't changed them. You have to admire that and I guess you take something from it too.

I knew the show in Vicar Street had gone well when it ended by the reception I got. I'd had a wedding gig in Galway the night before. Dad drove me down and coming home afterwards I was getting psyched up for Vicar Street. I was saying, 'This is it!' And Dad goes, 'Rory, you're well prepared.' And it was like having a chat with my dad on the way home from training before a big match with the club or the Meath minors.

I said, 'I have a vision of singing "Grace" at the end and the whole place hopping.'

He said, 'I hope it goes like that.'

At the end of the next night – we had a little party after – my dad came up to me.

'I have to say one thing, son, everything you said yesterday in the car was exactly what happened. It was just amazing to witness it.'

I always talk about mental health at the end of every show. I got a bit emotional because it was Vicar Street and what this meant for me and the journey I'd been on. St Declan's. Kiltale. The Chelsea Bell. Coogee Beach. Lahinch. All the things I'd been through and here I was standing before an audience of 900 at Vicar Street. I had followed my gut and my gut was true. Always trust your gut.

So, the show over, I told the audience that I needed to say a few things about mental health. The minute I mentioned this, one lad stood up in a Dublin jersey and went: 'Fucking love ya, Rory!'

I can't describe the full impact of that moment. It was unreal. I am fairly sure that this man had been through the mill. I choked up a bit and said that if I hadn't accepted and confronted my demons five years ago that I wouldn't be here. I told them to mind themselves. And then I signed off by singing 'Grace' with the warm-up band Blessed playing with me. It felt like there was a current going through my body.

The utter high of walking off that stage. I don't believe there's any drug that could match it. Before my show Foil, Arms & Hog, a popular comedy sketch act, were on stage and they were telling me they had done Vicar Street many times before. I could see that they were really professional and experienced and I had none of that behind me. They told me it didn't matter, that I had filled Vicar Street. 'They've come to see you. You've filled the place.' That gave me great confidence.

All my cousins were there after the show. I remember walking in and seeing Dave, my manager, and Tony, my trusted friend. My dad. Tony goes, 'Telling you now, every time I see you, you get better and better.'

I knew the show was strong. I'd been nationwide, performed it maybe 20 times. But this was the first at Vicar Street, so it was a landmark moment for me. Tony had been at many of my early shows in GAA clubs where I'd flopped on my hole. He was in The Chelsea Bell. I'd say he was very proud of me, thinking to himself, *That man absolutely died on his arse in New York and here he is three years later at a full Vicar Street.* Apart from Vicar Street the greatest buzz I've got from a show was after Dundalk, because I walked off stage feeling I'd done it, that's the fear gone. Now it's a case of getting better and better.

I looked at my Dad, Tony, and the others after the show, and said, 'Boys, that was unreal.' I knew my da was proud of me, he just couldn't say anything. It meant so much to me, because at the end of the day, I just want to make my family proud.

Emma, it goes without saying, has been my rock. My instincts were right. She has been instrumental in everything I've done. Whether it be after bad gigs or online abuse, she's always there. Likewise, when I'm flying too high, she has no problem bringing me back down. I went on an all-inclusive trip to Qatar a couple of years ago and for around four days I was treated like a king. I was brought over to provide entertainment at a GAA medals presentation, was put up in a savage hotel, wined and dined and waited on, the best of everything. I got home and I wasn't in the door an hour when she says, 'Get out and put those clothes on the line, you've been dilly-dallying for the last four days. And hoover the hall.' And that's what I love. Being brought down to earth like that. One day I'm being treated like royalty and the next I'm hanging out clothes in the back garden. She's good at keeping my feet on the ground.

I'm extremely proud of the kids, Ella and Zach. Ella is very much into her sport and dancing and Zach is a little terrier. And we're due another child in December. The house is going to get even noisier. I also managed to get a mortgage this year. Being self-employed, this was huge for me. So now I can provide a house for my family, a house that we can truly call home. My main aim is to make my children as proud of me as I can and if they struggle in later life I hope I can turn around and tell them, 'Well listen, I was there. I kept at it and I didn't give up.'

Because when I was younger I didn't really have anyone like that to look up to, that I could relate to. I love hearing stories of people who left school after third year and opened up their own business and became successful. These people should be going back into schools and talking more and giving people hope even though it's hardly the advice schools want to hear – that leaving school early is good for you. But I'm not advocating that. Nor am I advocating that the bright kids start getting kicked out of class. Just that we don't overlook or give up on those who find a different route. Education comes in many forms and those misfits who made good are the people we need to be hearing more from. There's always hope if you believe in yourself.

I hope people see me and my story as living proof that you can find what you are good at if you really want to. If you work hard you can achieve what you want in life. I try to set a good example every day so that those people struggling in school, or in jobs where they're not happy, can look at me and say, 'Well, Rory has no Leaving Cert, Rory wasn't good in school, Rory can't spell. But he's overcome all that. And I can too.'

Acknowledgements

I would like to thank all in Gill Books for helping me to produce this book. I would also like to thank Dermot Crowe for helping to capture my story. To anyone who had faith in me and, above all, to my family, thank you.